JUAN RAMÓN JIMÉNEZ
THREE HUNDRED POEMS, 1903–1953

Juan Ramón Jiménez
THREE HUNDRED
POEMS, 1903-1953

Translated by
ELOÏSE ROACH

INTRODUCTION BY RICARDO GULLÓN

UNIVERSITY OF TEXAS PRESS · AUSTIN

TO MY FATHER AND MOTHER

MR. AND MRS. J. A. ROACH

TRANSLATOR'S PREFACE

It seems to me that my life has been a pilgrimage on the trail of Juan Ramón Jiménez from the time at The University of Texas when, in courses taught by Miss Lilia Mary Casís, I first came across the now so-called "too romantic" *Pastorales* and *Eternidades*. From that time then—1924 or thereabouts—I read with excitement and delight anything that bore the magic name of Juan Ramón Jiménez: *Arias tristes, La soledad sonora, Diario de un poeta reciéncasado, Estío, Laberinto.* (Thirty years later I was amused and slightly nonplussed to find in the Zenobia-Juan Ramón Jiménez Library in the University of Puerto Rico a copy of *Laberinto* that had belonged to the poet with this note on the flyleaf in the poet's handwriting: "Este libro es muy malo. No debe leerse." [This book is very bad. It ought not to be read.] I learned from the curator of the Library, Miss Raquel Sárraga, and from Professor Gullón, who was engaged in editing the unpublished works of Juan Ramón, that Jiménez had tried to obtain and destroy all extant copies of this volume. He had been persuaded by friends to commute the death sentence of this copy, but he left it forever marked with his disapproval.)

In 1932 I had left the University and was teaching French and Spanish in the Stephen F. Austin State College in Nacogdoches when I accidentally discovered a thin little volume edited by Gertrude Walsh for beginning college students of Spanish: *Platero y yo*. Here I took up again the trail of Juan Ramón Jiménez. A painter friend, Allyn Gordon, and I spent many an excited Sunday reading to each other the 18 or 20 chapters of Miss Walsh's edition, and wishing for more. Having tasted *Platero*, I could not rest until I had the complete book. I ordered it and in due time received from the Residencia de Estudiantes in Madrid their 1932 edition. Then began more enchanted Sundays with the complete edition. And then began also the translation of the magical prose of Jiménez.

I do not remember how long it took me to translate forty or fifty chapters. I left Nacogdoches in 1933. By 1935 I must have had at least that many translated, for it was in that year that I asked and obtained permission from the poet to show him my version.

I am often asked, "Who introduced you to Jiménez?" Being ignorant of the greatness of the poet and of the necessity of having someone introduce me to him, I simply wrote him from Paris asking when he would see me. A telegram from him, July 25 at 7:20 A.M., gave me his address and telephone number. I arrived in Madrid the following day, stopping with friends at the Residencia de Estudiantes. There was a telephone message from Mrs. Jiménez: I was expected for lunch at one o'clock at 38 Padilla. Would I telephone?

I can still see myself in my white knitted suit and white shoes and hat and gloves, taking a taxi and being driven to 38 Padilla Street, entering through a huge iron grill-work gate, then through a huge doorway into a vestibule or foyer, up the elevator to the Jiménez apartment, ringing the doorbell, being met by a maid and ushered into a long living room. I can still see the long sofa, two or three armchairs and some straight chairs, all upholstered in purple damask. There was on one wall a lovely painting of the poet as a young man, which, they told me, had been painted by Sorolla when Juan Ramón was twenty-two years old. On another wall was a painting of Zenobia, also painted by Sorolla. He had done this portrait as a wedding gift. There was a long narrow table behind the long sofa. The two Jiménezes greeted me cordially. Zenobia spoke English beautifully—she was a graduate of Vassar. Juan Ramón and I spoke French to each other. Although Jiménez knew English, he did not feel at home speaking it; and although I knew Spanish, I felt reluctant to speak it to such a master, feeling myself more at ease in French. I don't remember what was served for lunch; but I remember the beautifully appointed table: the snow-white linen, the gleaming china and silver, the sparkling crystal. I also remember that the conversation during lunch centered around American poets; they wanted to know whether I knew their friend, Robert Frost, and another dear friend of theirs who had just died, Edwin Arlington Robinson; I remember being afraid they would out-do me in the knowledge of the poetry of these and other American writers.

After lunch we went to the living room where coffee and liqueur were served. Then the long table behind the long sofa was placed in front of it, and Jiménez and I spread out the pages of my translation upon it. Jiménez read and passed pages to Zenobia. When he had finished he told me he was happy with what I had done, and Zenobia had tears in her eyes. We went over the book chapter by chapter, and Jiménez chose some ninety chapters to be translated, saying that the others were too "anecdotical" and would hold no interest for the English-speaking reader. With his permission, his blessing, his encouragement, I returned to France and then to the United States.

In a ferment of high hopes I prepared and sent to publishers the ninety chapters, only to be disappointed over and over again. Even when the work was praised as "a really delightful work—very expertly translated," it was always returned. The last time it went out was in 1951. The editor wrote me a fine letter and asked to keep the manuscript a while. He hoped to convince his publisher that it would be worth publishing, but he did not succeed. Eventually he also sent it back, fortunately—as I now think—for all concerned. Only after the Nobel Prize had been conferred on Jiménez did I try again. This time I offered the manuscript to the University of Texas Press, and this time it was not rejected. *Platero and I* was published by the Press on August 19, 1957.

So came *Platero* to America, and here he has been welcomed and loved to the extent of six printings (the first edition of 5,000 copies was sold out in three weeks) and there still seems to be a demand for him.

But I was still on the trail of Juan Ramón Jiménez.

It had been my dream to go to Puerto Rico to visit the poet. That dream did not materialize, for he died May 29, 1958. In 1959 the Guggenheim Memorial Foundation granted me a fellowship for one year, September 1, 1959 to August 31, 1960, for the purpose of translating a representative collection of Jiménez's poetry. Since he and his wife had left to the University of Puerto Rico their library, his unpublished works, and their personal possessions, Puerto Rico was the ideal place for such a study.

I arrived there, in Pio Piedras, the second or third of September 1959. The following morning I went to find Connie Saleva, administrative assistant to the Rector of the University, Dr. Benítez, and former secretary of Juan Ramón Jiménez. She gave me a friendly welcome and took me to the Zenobia–Juan Ramón *Sala* in the University Library. The University is a very attractive place and its Library, a modern spacious building. A large room or hall in it was dedicated, while both Mr. and Mrs. Jiménez were living, as library-museum to house the poet's library, his own works, and other memorabilia of the famous couple.

As I entered the Zenobia-Juan Ramón room, time rolled back, and I was again in the living room of 38 Padilla in Madrid. Here were the long sofa and arm chairs and straight chairs upholstered in purple damask—the same purple damask, only slightly faded. Here were the two Sorolla paintings facing each other from opposite walls, and the long library table on which the poet and I had placed the pages of my translation of *Platero and I*. I went to stand by a large showcase in which rested the death mask of the poet, a cast of his right hand, and the Nobel diploma and gold medal. Here was the end of the trail.

Miss Saleva introduced the curator of the *Sala*, Miss Raquel Sárraga, and Professor Ricardo Gullón, who came from Spain in 1954 to interview Jiménez for a book on *Modernísmo* and remained to teach in the University. (The resultant book, *Conversaciones con Juan Ramón*, gives delightful side lights of the poet's life in Puerto Rico as well as fine insight into his work and thoughts.) At the time I met Professor Gullón, he was engaged in editing the poet's unpublished works and teaching Spanish literature in the University. Miss Saleva, Miss Sárraga, and Mr. Gullón took great interest in what I was to do and gave me generously of their time and friendship. Here in the *Sala* I was to feel again the spirit of Zenobia and Juan Ramón; the whole atmosphere of the place was one of closeness to them. Here were the books that they had handled and read, often marked in their handwriting; the books that they had written together or separately; and such personal objects as Zenobia's fans and handkerchiefs (and her honorary membership card in Father Flanagan's Boystown), and the little pebbles from Moguer that Juan Ramón always carried in his pocket and fingered constantly. In addition I was also to hear the poet's voice again. Zenobia had had the foresight to bring to the classroom where he lectured a tape recorder; and one may sit in the hall and hear the slightly dry, soft yet forceful voice of Juan Ramón Jiménez discussing *Modernismo*.

So I followed the trail of Juan Ramón Jiménez through his books, his writings, his magazines and magazine articles; through conversations with his friends, his fellow faculty-members, his admirers; but especially through his poems. I believe I read every poem he ever wrote which was published, and several different versions of many of them. As I read, the plan for the present anthology began slowly to take shape.

Mr. Jiménez had specifically requested that none of his poems earlier than 1903 be reproduced. He himself had chosen from time to time what he considered his best work and had had it published in anthologies. In addition, he had published a last anthology, *Tercera antolojía poética,* which was the selection, according to the poet's handwritten note on the title page, of Zenobia. Often in these different anthologies or in different printings of them, the poet made changes in the poems. Sometimes the changes involve only a word or the position of a word; at other times they may involve the addition or the elimination of several lines or of a whole stanza. Wishing to remain as close as possible to the poet's own preferred version of the poems, I chose, whenever I could, the versions in these three anthologies. Occasionally, however, I preferred a version in the first or second anthology, or in the original volume, to his latest choice in the third. Such is the case in "Mañana de la cruz," which he changed to "Mañana de la luz."

All but sixteen of the poems in the present collection were taken from these anthologies and from the Nobel Prize collection, *Libros de poesía,* which includes in one volume the nine books published by the poet from 1914 to 1949. The excepted sixteen came from books published from 1903 to 1914, and from *Canción, En el otro costado,* and *Romances de Coral Gables.*

What determined the inclusion of these particular poems rather than any other 300 from the 2,500 or so read? No doubt personal preference weighed heavily, but my first consideration was to give a comprehensive view of the poet's work, an adequate perspective of the continuous development of fifty years of his poetry, from the youthful work of 1903 to the achievement of his ideal of "naked poetry" (*poesía desnuda, mía para siempre*).

Almost as important, it has seemed to me, is to keep the form of each poem, conserving as far as possible the rhythm and the rhyme or assonance of the original without destroying its spirit, its essential meaning. This was impossible in many cases (given the great difference between the two languages), particularly when a word of like Latin extraction did not seem to fit the meaning as closely as one of Anglo-Saxon origin. Juan Ramón Jiménez, having himself struggled to render English into Spanish, would, I hope, forgive such lapses.

I wish to acknowledge with gratitude my indebtedness to the following persons whose help and interest in one way or another made possible the completion of this work: the

John Guggenheim Memorial Foundation, Henry Allen Moe, Secretary, for the fellowship that gave me a year's freedom for the necessary research; Jaime Benítez, Rector of the University of Puerto Rico, for permission to work in the Sala Zenobia-Juan Ramón Jiménez; Miss Raquel Sárraga, Curator of the Sala, and Professor Ricardo Gullón, editor of Juan Ramón Jiménez's unpublished works, who with unfailing helpfulness placed at my disposal all available materials for my task; Miss Connie Saleva, administrative assistant to the Rector of the University of Puerto Rico and former secretary of Juan Ramón Jiménez, through whose good offices all arrangements with the University of Puerto Rico were made; George Schade, for his careful reading of the manuscript and invaluable suggestions for revisions; and to Francisco Hernández-Pinzón Jiménez for permission to publish these poems.

ELOÏSE ROACH

CONTENTS

Translator's Preface vii

Introduction xvii

Arias tristes 3

Jardines lejanos 9

Pastorales 13

Olvidanzas 25

Baladas de primavera 27

Elejías 31

La soledad sonora 33

Poemas májicos y dolientes 35

Arte menor 37

Poemas agrestes 39

Laberinto 41

Melancolía 43

Poemas impersonales 45

Apartamiento 49

La frente pensativa 53

Pureza 55

Sonetos espirituales 59

Estío 73

Diario de un poeta reciéncasado . . . 87

Eternidades 107

Piedra y cielo 123

Poesía (en verso) 137

Belleza (en verso) 147

Canción 159

La estación total I 167

Canciones de la nueva luz 175

La estación total II 189

En el otro costado 193

Romances de Coral Gables 199

Animal de fondo 203

Dios deseado y deseante 229

Ríos que se van 233

Index of Titles and First Lines

Spanish 235

English 250

INTRODUCTION

Juan Ramón Jiménez lived for poetry and in it he found the road to perfection, the yearning and yearned-for god whose embrace can give meaning to life and to death. He was born in Moguer, a small town in lower Andalusia, close to the port of Palos, on the Atlantic coast, from which four centuries before Columbus' caravels had sailed: white houses, narrow, sun-bright streets, children with large dark eyes, a town-crier's call from afar, the clattering oxcarts, the rock-rose, and by night the intense sweet odor of the night-blooming dondiego. Born on December 23, 1881, (although he—the Christmas-child to his mother—preferred to designate the evening of the 24th as the moment of his arrival in the world), he had a carefree, happy childhood; in his early youth he went to Seville to study law (fate of the majority of Spanish youths at that time), to please his father; and to paint, to please himself.

His juridical career was cut short by a failure in a history examination, and his inclination toward painting was not long in giving way to the poetic vocation. The father, ill for a long time, died suddenly in his sleep, and the memory of that sad night grew in the anguish of the son until it became immense and deep, like eternity. It was a memory that decided his character, for the emotional shock suffered when his sister awoke him to tell him the father had died filled him forever with melancholy and presentiment. He imagined himself marked for the same fate and believed that his heart would fail him at any moment. He wrote his first books and published them in 1900, after a brief first trip to Madrid, but the morbid terror of sudden death became an obsession (and gave rise to a kind of self-pity); seeking diversion and rest he lived for a year in the French sanatorium of Le Bouscat (Bordeaux). He lived, that is, he wrote a little, he read a great deal from the modern poets of that country—Baudelaire, Verlaine, Albert Samain, Francis Jammes . . . and he fell in love, or thought himself in love, with several girls that chance placed in his path.

A short stay in the Castilian country finished restoring his strength and (as he used to say) brought him new books, sentimental ones, but not like his rimes of his French lonely days: *Arias tristes, Pastorales*, and, between those two, *Jardines lejanos,* with its veilings of mystery. Brought him, I say, because Juan Ramón felt his intuitions turn into poems with the spontaneity of a natural phenomenon, as if dictated by the loving hand of the muse. In our day, inspiration is in bad repute, and he who invokes it risks being thought retrograde and poorly informed. Reversing a sentence of Paul Valéry's we might affirm that if daily work provides the last thirteen lines of a sonnet, the first line is born from inspiration and only from it.

Juan Ramón thought that poetry is emanation secretly and silently rising within the poet, as water in the rock, with the spontaneousness of a spring whose existence reveals a subterranean stream; an interior current, no doubt, in this poet to whom Rubén Darío said: "You live inwardly." The beauty of the countryside, the peace of village life, the sadness of old parks, the evocation of exotic or impossible images, hallucinations . . . stimulated in this first epoch the poet's inclination toward melancholy, transparently declared in the titles of some of his works. Because he was sentimental and nostalgic for the past, the critics, needing a label to catalogue him, called him decadent. He and his friends recognized themselves as "modernists," and the label prevailed: in the Spanish-speaking countries modernism was the name given to the reforming literary movement headed by Darío. Now we see it as a time comprising distinct tendencies: Parnasianism and Symbolism, exotism and indigenism coinciding paradoxically as forms of evasion and protest against the vertical invasion of the dense municipal world stigmatized by Rubén Darío. In art, to be a modernist was equivalent to considering the accepted social values outworn and old-fashioned and to postulating a total renovation of thought and attitudes. Modernism was anticonformist, and in the "angry young men" of the present, last heirs of the courteous rebels of yesterday, we find the disorbited and spectacular prolongation of the derangement initiated in such inoffensive books as *Prosas profanas,* of Darío, or *Ninfeas,* of Juan Ramón.

In the origins of modernism, currents of diverse sources had their influence: romantic heritage and liberal tradition, a return to the past and a withdrawal in distance, antidogmatic inclination and a desire to "modernize" religious dogma—that is, to make it flexible. (In the poem music was desirable, but not above all things—only one of them.) If the form was to be sculptured and beautiful, it was still required, more imperatively, to keep it ductile and sinuous the better to mold it to the fluid course of intuition.

The secret galleries of the soul and the roads of dreams were not the exclusive domain of Antonio Machado—another of the great poets of Spain of this century—for Juan

Ramón traveled along them and found, in the shadow, illuminations that make us feel the presence of mysterious realities, working in some manner in the being. The consciousness of mystery, the sensation of mystery, imposes itself without excess, without melodrama, and faces the reader with the final interrogations, as Unamuno summarized them: What is time that makes us or destroys us and how does it pass—or stay? Is not living but un-living? Is man something more than shadow or dream? Are we a dream of God or is He dreamed by us? Is poetry a miraculous capturing of the eternal in the instant?

Settled in Madrid from 1902, Juan Ramón had a part in the publication and in the direction of a notable literary magazine: *Helios*, in which the young men of that time appeared in militant, fervent, enthusiastic, and impassioned groups. The poet lived for a while in the Rosario Sanatorium, this time not because of illness but to find in such surroundings a solitude conducive to work. One day (1906), perhaps because he felt sad, he decided to return to "the white marvel" of his native town, not so much to live it as to dream it and to construct a Moguer of the imagination that, being a reflection of the real Moguer, should transcend it. His poetic world was inhabited by the "beings and ghosts" of the past, of childhood, figures that had existed (and perhaps existed still) and that, enhanced by the transfiguring magic of nostalgia with nothing spectral in their outlines, drew him toward the past. He lived in the present, but starting from yesterday.

His solitude was a labyrinth populated by images and not lacking communication with the outer world. As an artist devoted to creativity, he lived absorbed in thought, considering creativity his reason for being, better still, his very being, and defending it from disturbing intrusions. He was a solitary, but not an exile from life, and in the Moguer solitude a little donkey, with whom he carried on conversations as one converses with nature, accompanied him for hours. That little donkey, named Platero, grazes immortal in the green meadows of the Elysian Fields, beside Rocinante and Rucio, the faithful companions of Don Quixote and Sancho.

His dialogue with nature, enriching the constant spinning of the creative imagination, was crystalized in that admirable work (*Platero y yo,* 1914), lyrical biography, collection of etchings, Andalusian elegy . . . Yes, Andalusian and universal, as the author wanted it, striving to achieve universality by reaching into his own depth until he could touch the most particular and local, the essential human. He concentrated on the simple incidents of living, in the bare instant, to the point of not dividing his life into days, but his day into lives: "each day, each hour, an entire life." Such concentration gave his poetry density and intensity: in each line we feel him complete, gravitating above it with all the weight of his soul and of his dream—lucid dream of deep realities, penetration into the other face of reality, to the point of converting the temporal into substance of the eternal and the limited into expression of the infinite. To give himself up to poetry was to give himself up to life, to life each day different and the same, like daybreak; to life at its deepest level, with the bird and the rose, the child and the cloud. From Unamuno he learned to consider life as a succession of imperishable moments, for, as the great Rector of the University of Salamanca used to say, "He who does not have the intuition of the momentaneity of everything living is not a true artist." And Juan Ramón saw the world in its natural dynamism, things in their unceasing transformation, and he transferred them to the poem with the conviction that by placing them therein he was destining them to eternity.

In 1912 he returned to Madrid and made the acquaintance of Zenobia Camprubí Aymar, whom he was later to marry. Before meeting her, Juan Ramón had felt vaguely in love with two or three fragile, ethereal, dreamy women with whose nature and sensibility his coincided, or he thought his coincided—romantic loves, somewhat literary, half invented, in which love was as important or perhaps more important than the loved one. With Zenobia, practical, efficient, gay, everything was otherwise: the differences were as evident as the affinities, but passion overtook the poet, who struggled to win her love, came down from the clouds, and succeeded in convincing the realist that, if not on poetry, it was possible to live with and in poetry. After a period of hesitation and doubt, Zenobia agreed, and their first joint enterprise was the translation from English to Spanish of the Hindu poet Rabindranath Tagore. Zenobia Camprubí was bilingual, as she had lived for years in the United States, where her brothers, American citizens, lived. One of them, José Camprubí, came to be well known in New York, especially in the Spanish-American *milieu,* as founder and director of the daily, *La Prensa.*

Toward the end of 1915, Zenobia came with her mother to New York and Juan Ramón was not long in following her. They were married on Thursday, March 2, 1916, in the Roman Catholic Church of St. Stephen. In an article published two years before her death she recalled how, on leaving the City Hall, where they had gone to obtain the marriage license, they met a "plump Irish policeman," who with his index finger on high, warned them: "You'd better look out! It is easier to get in than to get out!" They never had to get out, and in his wife the poet found the ideal companion: spirited and enterprising friend, wise counselor, efficient secretary, and even chauffeur. Thanks to her uninterrupted watchfulness, this man, so little practical, was able to devote himself to writing without preoccupying himself with any problem whatsoever. She would resolve them in her discreet and able fashion, removing from the horizon the small daily clouds.

The trip to the United States inspired a book which he wrote from day to day: *Diario de un poeta reciéncasado.* The movement of the sea—affirmed Juan Ramón—gave his verse a different rhythm, a fluidity and freedom which not only changed his poetry, but had their influence in the total scope of the Spanish tongue. Never, in this language, had free verse been so totally free—free verse and admirable prose (no less poetic) to tell the impressions of the soul enriched by love and by the sea. In the preliminary foreword he placed this revealing confession: "The heart, if it exists, is always the same; silence—true universal language and golden!—is the same everywhere." The external happening will not affect the essential, for under the changing spectacle it is possible to recognize the law of unity and identity that governs the universe.

Faced with the North American spectacle he was not to seek the picturesque, but the eternal. That does not mean, as obtuse critics insinuated, that he was incapable of grasping and understanding the novelties that he met in the course of his trip. He understood them and he expressed them, and with them the murmur of the permanent. There are in the *Diario* poems which are images of the North American reality as he saw it, without distortion of the appearance, but with a glance curious to discover the vibration, the illuminating gleam which would give him the clue to a people and a form which were to him at once strange and familiar. By a queer paradox, this Juan Ramón, accused of living in the high tower of his indifference to the world, was able to see the United States, then and later, without ballast, saying what was observed with more exactness than the magical Federico García Lorca, visionary who saw a nightmare New York.

On his return from the United States, and almost at the same time as the *Diario* (1917), Juan Ramón published another of his great books, *Sonetos espirituales*. If the former represents in his work the beginning of a second manner, the latter closes the first phase with such perfection that that very completeness justifies the change. It did not seem possible to go any further along the way of formal severity resplendent in those poems that the poet called "interior," perhaps because, as the critic Díez Canedo observed, they are written "from within outward" discarding the "exterior" brilliance and sonority of the baroque and romantic sonnets. Technically they make use of devices of immense variety: internal rhymes, images in series, a single figure prolonged throughout the fourteen lines, pointillism, alliterations, sounds cooperating with the expression, the play of antitheses, enumerations and reiterations . . . Juan Ramón thought that he had exhausted exquisiteness and preciosity and, not wishing to repeat himself, to plagiarize himself, he changed course.

The years from 1916 to 1936 were years of ceaseless creativity and of critical revision of earlier poetry. He "relived" his poems daily. The anthology published by the Hispanic Society and later the popular one by Espasa Calpe, together with the editions of *Platero y yo*, which at that time were being multiplied, spread the work of the poet in new circles. He dedicated his poems to the minority, but to the "immense minority" capable of feeling the beauty of the world, and not to minuscule groups of the initiated. Nothing in his work was inaccessible—nor even difficult—for people able to enjoy beauty; nothing esoteric, nor cryptic, nor distant, for Juan Ramón wrote at the level of the heart.

Esoterism, no; compulsion and anxiety for pureness, yes: poetry without concession to the ideological or verbal commonplace (and the one is usually accompanied by the other) and conviction that to write poetry is to tell truth and in truth, to express in direct and meaningful fashion profound realities that it is not possible to communicate otherwise. He had a consciousness of mission, a feeling that his role as poet consisted in revealing the inexpressible, putting into words the dark intimation, the fragrance that fleetingly crosses the human heart. Influenced by the teacher's theory of his friend, the great educator Francisco Giner de los Ríos, founder of the Free Institution of Teaching, he made his own ethic of vocation, and he devoted himself to his own poetical and poetizing task with absolute dedication: "my relation with poetry"—he said—"is a passionate one," and the consciousness of mission inclined him to be satisfied only with perfection.

Ethic and esthetic were closely associated in his ideology. He published some aphorisms under the title *Estética y ética estética* thus declaring the evident relation between the moral and the beautiful. When he writes: "for me there are no other reasons in life—nor in death—than esthetic reasons," he is not adopting the attitude of the esthetic devotee of art for art's sake but enunciating the will to adjust conduct and life to the line of purity and austerity preached by Giner—to the example.

Juan Ramón was contributing, in his fashion and with his means, to the general labor of bestirring the national conscience to which at that time the best Spaniards, eager to pull their country out of the abyss of vulgarity and bungling into which the relaxation of the creative potentials and the abdication of intellectual effort had led her, were dedicated. A political labor, certainly, but in the noblest sense of the word, for they wanted to create a new type of man able to coexist in common enterprises, subordinating himself to them and bringing to fruition with patient love the tasks, however slight, entrusted to his care: to place the stones one on the other, being careful to raise a solid wall, for perhaps the finished work will be a cathedral destined to soar.

As Unamuno did, as Ortega, Juan Ramón insisted on emphasizing the importance of work well done, but his efforts remained in the scope of poetry, gaining in intensity what they lost in extent. As against the academic and literary-contest rhetoricians, as against the doubtful professional patriots who were satisfied with proclaiming the glories of the past, exalting "casticism" as a way of life, Juan Ramón practiced the estheticism of creativeness, the rigors of exactness and, when necessary, the subtle exercise of criticism. The best were with him, and the development of the literary generation of the twenties was Ortegan and Juan-Ramonian. Without violating their loyalty to their innate diversity, the young poets followed the example of vocational ethics proposed by the author of *Diario*. García Lorca, Jorge Guillén, Rafael Alberti . . . , in addition to receiving the impact of Juan-Ramonian poetry, lived the creativeness with authenticity, risking their fate on this card. Juan Ramón called them to collaborate in the fine and short-lived literary magazines which he edited at that time: *Indice, Ley* and *Sí.*

Life impelled Juan Ramón to extend the radius of his works, and in 1935–1936 his contributions to the press became frequent; not until June of 1936, a month before the beginning of the Spanish Civil War, did he consent to give lectures, and, as a matter of fact, the first one, announced to be given in the Students' Residence (Residencia de Estudiantes) with the title of "Política poética," he did not give: overcome at the last moment by doubts and worries about his ability to do it, he delegated the task to a friend.

The war, and more than that the Civil War, had inevitably to wound the poet as it did: in the first weeks of the struggle he established and directed in Madrid, with his wife, a small children's refuge, for nothing moved him so much as the effect of the war on the children; later, the Republican government separated him from the struggle by naming him honorary cultural attaché in the United States. In September 1936 Zenobia and Juan Ramón returned to this country (Cherbourg to New York, the transatlantic vessel *Aquitania*, a sad crossing, almost without seeing the sea, memory fixed on the "distant land driven insane"), beginning a long peregrination through the Western Hemisphere, which they would never again leave except in death. For the temporary removal was to become definitive, altering substantially the life of the couple, and not only through the geographical transplanting, but also inasmuch as it led to a total change in their habits. The necessity of reconstructing their life forced them into new activities. It was necessary to work and Juan Ramón decided to accept an offer to lecture in Puerto Rico and in Cuba. Success persuaded him that he could communicate directly with the public, bringing him close to a world from which until then he had remained apart, the university world. In 1939, the Jiménezes went to Florida, settling in Coral Gables, Miami, both having been invited by the University to take part in the work of the Hispanic American Institute. In the meetings held in 1940 and 1942 Juan Ramón participated, giving three lectures in each of them; in 1942 he moved to Duke University, North Carolina, as professor of the Spanish School, in the summer session, and not only to lecture but also to hold conversations with students in afternoon parties and meetings, awakening or quickening their interest in poetry.

In Coral Gables Juan Ramón wrote a series of excellent "interior" lyrics and a long poem (his longest), *Espacio*, which he published first in verse and later in prose, attempting to erase in the presentation of poetry differences which he believed purely visual, accidental in relation to the substance of what was expressed and the rhythm with which it was expressed. *Espacio* is a lyrical meditation inspired by the intuition of life in its development, of the changeable and of the permanent as it gradually forms us, molds us. Life is movement in space (in the space of time) and if movement ceases, life ends. Past, present, and presentiment fused in the surge of memory and of imagination, or, if you prefer, of the remembering imagination which corresponds to the imaginative memory as the obverse to the reverse of a coin. The peninsula of Florida, as he was careful to make clear, the vast coral reef, with its limitless horizons, with its prolonged multicolored beauty, inspired in him this open, free, unending poem, and the rich variations and resonances in which he summarized the best of his vital and poetic experiences.

Zenobia began teaching in the University of Maryland and the couple moved to Riverdale, whose elm trees the poet sang and used as a title of a book—*Los olmos de Riverdale*—announced, but never published. There he developed a friendship with his neighbor, a farmer and religious man; one day he learned with surprise that that fervent horticulturist was the vice-president of the United

States: Henry A. Wallace. Impressed by the simplicity of character and the rectitude of his neighbor's intentions, he dedicated to him a delightful article in which he called him "an artisan toward God," showing him as the idealist (American Quixote) to whom the ideal appears as something tangible, realizable in the present and not in a nebulous future.

During the World War, Juan Ramón tried to cooperate, as far as possible for him, with the liberating effort of the Allies, and by invitation from the Coordinator's Office in Washington, he gave several radio lectures directed principally to listeners in Spanish America. In the first of these he declared: "Since 1939 I have been living in these United States, where moral and physical freedom are still respected. I like to live in the country of Freedom for I have been, am, and wish to be until the end, a free man ."

Unexpectedly the fears of his early youth returned and with them the obsession with death. He was hospitalized in the Washington Sanatorium and Hospital, in Takoma Park, where he was treated for an attack of depression similar to those suffered half a century before. There, little by little, he recovered and was able to work; the songs of Takoma remain in his work to prove it.

He missed his native tongue, he needed to hear Spanish all around, conversation, murmur, prayer, and song; he needed to hear it in the streets, filtering through walls, to smell it . . . For it is from the living tongue, the one heard and spoken constantly in mutation and in permanence, that poetry is nurtured. In August 1948 he traveled (his fourth long sea voyage) to the countries of the river Plata: Argentina and Uruguay, to discover with incredulous surprise that he, poet of the minority, artist of a few, according to what the dull-witted so often repeated, was welcomed by multitudes with the clamor and hysteria generally reserved for the sport or screen star. The enthusiasm of the general public made him realize the extent of his popularity, for the people filled the halls of the theatres where he lectured, overran hallways and points of vantage, and on some occasions even interfered with street traffic.

The multitudinous success, with the usual paraphernalia of autograph hunters, newspaper interviews, sticky visitors, and admirers that follow the current neither dazzled him nor even impressed him; applause could not alter the quality of his poetic work, the only thing that truly mattered to him. And thus he returned to his work with the feeling, experienced for the second time, that the sea trip had contributed in some fashion to the renovation of his poetry, spurring him at this juncture to face decisively the radical theme of his work: that of the god-poetry, *Animal de fondo* yearned-for and yearning, in whom throbs the divine submerged in the soul and resplendent outside of it "like a single consciousness, just, universal, of the beauty that is within us and without us at the same time." Poetry-consciousness-light of God and thanks to it total possession of the world, penetration into the mystery, exploration of the I and of its innumerable subtleties and complications, *Animal de fondo* is possibly the last great symbolist book of our century, in the tradition of Stefan George and W. B. Yeats (whom Juan Ramón annotated and translated).

The poet feels poetry as an emanation of the divinity, of the creative ferment that inhabits him and is at once something his own and something strange to him, in absolute identification, as that of "fire with its air." The world is transformed in possession and the poetical objects acquire relevance on being inscribed within a series of images that try to suggest the presence of that god possible and revealed by poetry and in poetry.

In 1951 he fell again into depression and, trying to relieve him, Zenobia decided to live in some Spanish-speaking place. They accepted the invitation of the University of Puerto Rico, moving to the Island, quiet water, a perhaps artificial and dissonant parenthesis in the festering wound of the contemporary world; land on the margin of chaos, ignorant of the prophecies, of the apocalypse announced for day after tomorrow, that constitutes itself into an oasis possible or impossible, brief paradise in which it is still possible to sing and laugh without a feeling of guilt. Juan Ramón had pleasant memories of the months he had lived there in 1936, and although things had changed (for television, the sociologists, and Mr. Hilton break into all paradises), the atmosphere in which the Jiménezes moved continued essentially the same. The decision was a wise one, for Juan Ramón was not long in recovering to the extent that he was able to prepare and teach a course on literary modernism, a theme on which he could speak as participant and witness, and not just as a teacher. He felt at home, surrounded by friends and students interested in his work, sharers in the same tradition and often with identical ideals. The old poet attended concerts, visited schools to enjoy the company of Puerto-Rican children, and devoted hours and hours to the reading of the poems of beginning writers, in order to encourage them, selecting the outstanding ones and publishing them in the literary pages of the student magazine, *Universidad*, which through his influence reserved enough space for poetry. In these pages the master took his turn with the youth, and, next to theirs, texts by well-known Spanish and Spanish-American writers were inserted.

The years of exile led Juan Ramón to an examination of conscience and to the expounding of his ideas on the obsessive themes of the times. "Política Poética," the 1936 lecture whose title he changed to "El trabajo gustoso," had been a sort of rough draft of his "political" preoccupation, later depurated into "Aristocracia y democracia," "La razón heróica" and other essays. The Platonic idea of total harmony—not only concord but a fusion between men and the world around—was not new to him, for, during the years 1910–1911, it had inspired poems unequivocally drawn under the influence of Plato; but previously he had never taken the trouble of systematizing his ideas as he attempted to do in the American lectures.

For him, to be an aristocrat was "to rise or attempt to rise into a being which we must all be creating, for we aspire to create and are creating our superior I, our best descendant." Democracy seemed to him a link for reaching the aristocratic status of justice and final harmony, a means and not an end. The terms *aristocracy* and *democracy* did not have in his vocabulary the meanings given in political science treatises: the Juan-Ramonian vision of the problems of coexistence were cultural and "poetical"; he denied that those terms were antithetical, and in his system they were not contradictory since he considered democracy as the "organism builder of total superior life without individual egoism."

In the last twenty years of his life he wrote excellent literary essays on Edgar Allan Poe, the Spanish romantic Gustavo Adolfo Bécquer, and on the Cuban poet Eugenio Florit; he discussed in Spanish lyric poetry two permanent lines of creativeness: closed poetry and open poetry, parallel opposition to the one already indicated by him between literature and poetry; he made a thorough study of the "romance," which he called "river of the Spanish tongue," and devoted a good deal of his time to the writing of the history of modernism and to the analysis of it as of the old world and of the new. In his youth he had published articles of literary criticism, but he soon interrupted that activity not to resume it until his settling in America, where the horizon of his interest widened so greatly.

If his poetry reached in *Espacio* and in *Animal de fondo* an impressive lyrical and metaphysical density, his prose matured to the point of imaginative precision and verbal certainty evident in the fabulous portraits of *Españoles de tres mundos* (Europe, America, and Death), written over a period of forty years; in them the metaphor becomes an instrument to reveal the identity of the person without once falling into the commonplace, nor being led, by an understandable reaction against the topic, to the enervated and false figure of speech. The style gradually grew more flexible and at the same time more temperate: ideas are expressed with fluency and exactness, associated and even in series without impairing the verbal economy and the sobriety in the use of adjectives. Because of aversion to the sentimentality of his youth, in his maturity he inclined toward rigorous contemplation, and at times to caricature, of the world and of people.

In 1952 Zenobia fell ill and physicians diagnosed cancer. She fought valiantly, she spent time on several occasions in hospitals, she underwent various treatments, and in 1956 accepted uncomplainingly the idea of the proximity of death, affirming that the good of such an insidious illness is that it permits the patient to adjust the time table of the last tasks, devoted, in this case to leaving Juan Ramón's affairs thoroughly in order for the time when she would not be there. Three days before her death, a friend took to the hospital where Zenobia was dying the news of the awarding of the Nobel Prize to Juan Ramón; on learning it, incapable of speech, she hummed without words a song learned in childhood. She died on the twenty-eighth of October, and Juan Ramón, whose strength was failing, felt his life ended. He still succeeded in recovering, but he never wrote again. He suffered an accident that made him an invalid and he died in Puerto Rico the twenty-ninth of May 1958.

RICARDO GULLÓN

Translation of Eloïse Roach

JUAN RAMÓN JIMÉNEZ
THREE HUNDRED POEMS, 1903–1953

ARIAS TRISTES (1902–1903)

1

River of crystal, asleep
and enchanted; gentle valley,
gentle riverbanks filled with
white poplars and green-leaved willows.

—The valley has a daydream
and a heart; it dreams and knows
how to fashion with its dream
languid sound of flutes and songs—

Enchanted river; the drowsy
branches of the willow trees
falling in the quiet pools
are kissing the limpid crystals.

And the sky is soft and placid,
a low and floating sky,
that with its silvery mist
caresses the waves and trees.

3

My heart often has dreamed of
the riverbank and the valley,
and has come to this serene,
quiet shore to embark;
but coming along the path
it has wept for love because
of an old love song it heard
coming from another valley.

2

My soul is kin to the gray
sky and the withered leaves.
Inward-turning autumn sun,
do not touch me with your grief.

—The trees in the garden are
heavily laden with mist.
My heart divines among them
the lover it cannot find;
and in the wet ground dry leaves
open withered hands to me.
If only my soul could be
a leaf lost among these leaves!

The sun has sent down a ray
of strange gold to the trees,
a floating sunbeam, a soft
light for the secret things.

—What tenderness in the last
sunlight for the dying leaves!
An endless harmony strays
slowly along the paths,
an eternal symphony
of music and fragrances
that goldens the garden with
a more divine spring.

And that light of mist and gold,
passing through the withered leaves,
creates in my heart a rainbow
of vague, hidden loveliness.

3

(Le vent de l'autre nuit a jeté
bas l'Amour . . . P. Verlaine)

Late one afternoon the wind
swept away so many leaves!
How saddened the trees must be
on this night without stars!

I left my window ajar.
—The moon moves along as dead,
unlighted by kiss or tears,
yellow-looking in the fog.

And I have caressed the trees
with glances of tenderness,
making the tiny soft-green
leaves of spring open wide.

Are they perhaps dreaming so
of their poor dead leaves?
I say to them: "Do not weep;
they'll come back with the new leaves."

4
I Shall Not Return

I shall not return. And night,
mildly warm, serene and silent,
will lull the world, under beams
of its solitary moon.

My body will not be there,
and through the wide-open window,
a refreshing breeze will come
inquiring for my soul.

I don't know if any await
the end of my double absence,
or who will kiss my memory
amidst caresses and weeping.

But there will be stars and flowers,
there will be sighs and hopes,
and love in the avenues
in the shadows of the trees.

And that piano will be playing
as in this untroubled night,
and no one there to listen,
pensive, by my window frame.

5

Stars, stars, sweet stars,
sorrowful, distant stars,
are you the eyes of dead friends?
—You gaze with such fixity!
Are you the eyes of dead friends
now remembering the earth
—O bright flowers of the soul—
with the newly-come spring?

6

The moon sends into my deep
soul a rain of dazzlement
that leaves it exactly like
a gracious fresh-water well.

Then my depths, benign to all,
well upward and upward swell,
opening their sparkling fountain
at the level of the world.

Water that joins star and flower,
excites thirst with heavenly fires
where, like shipwrecks of love,
the kingdoms of blue are lying.

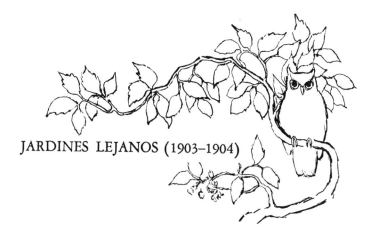

JARDINES LEJANOS (1903–1904)

7

I go to the garden. Women!
Wait for me! Wait! And my love
grasps an arm. Come! Who are you?
And I see it is a flower!

By the fountain! Yes, it's they!
Wait for me, wait, woman, wait!
... I grasp at the water. Stars
that one cannot ever hold!

8

Early Morning

(Tryst)

The wind is bending the branches
laden with sleeping birds.
—The lighthouse opens its green
eye three times—The crickets hush.

How far the hurricane puts
places, one from another!
How difficult what was easy!
How impassable the roads!

Everything seems interchanged.
But in the intimate light
the sands and the flowers are
where we saw them last evening.

9

Is it I, pacing my room
tonight, or is it the tramp
who was prowling in my garden
at the fall of dusk?

                    I look
around and find everything
is the same and not the same . . .
Was the window left wide open?
Had I not fallen asleep?
Was not the garden in green
of moonlight? . . . The sky was clear
and blue . . . Now there are clouds and wind

and all the garden is dark . . .
I believe my beard was
black . . . And I was wearing gray.
And now my beard is white
and I wear mourning. Is this
my walk? Does this voice
I now utter have the rhythms
of the voice I used to have?
Am I myself, or am I
the beggar prowling my garden
at the fall of night?

I look
around . . . There are clouds and winds . . .
The garden is full of gloom . . .

. . . I walk up and down . . . Had I
already fallen asleep?
My beard is white . . . All things
are the same and not the same.

10

When woman is present, all
things are serene, themselves
—the flame, the flower, and song—
But whenever woman leaves
—the light, the song, and the flame—
everything, crazily, is she.

Who is walking up the road
this late evening, gardener?
—There is no one on the road . . .
—Perhaps an ill-omened bird.

A red owl or a jackdaw,
twin eyes of the pelican . . .
—It is the end of the rain
in the solitary field. . . .

—Gardener, it is not the rain,
it is not the rain . . . —My word,
it is the rain, gentle sir.
—It must be the rain of death.

Gardener, didn't you hear
a voice from the balcony?
—Gentle sir, it is the beat
of your very own heart.

—When will the morning return
bringing rosy happiness?
When will the bells start ringing
to say "good morning, good day"?

I hear a dragging chain,
a hollow voice, it is . . .
—Gentle sir, it is the dogs,
the dogs baying at the moon . . .

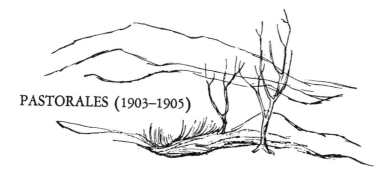

PASTORALES (1903–1905)

12

The countryside sleeps, trembling
in its own celestial sadness,
to the music that is made
by the crickets and the stars.

The distant horizon turns,
the hill runs away, the valley
shivers, the path disappears . . .
and all in the soft
clarity of the new moon . . .

Who went by? I do not know . . .
There along the high road
tinkle the harness bells
of a stagecoach coming close;

fantastic coach, nocturnal
carriage that never arrives . . .
—No . . . it is only the music
of the crickets and the stars.

Was it the river? the breeze?
the running water that grieves?
flowers with their shattered crowns,
the voice of the miller's wife . . .

Is it love passing? Oh, love!
it is the calm drowsy water
inviting down to its depth
of crystal, shadow, and grass.

—No . . . it is the water quivering
and blue with moonlight, atremble
to the music that is made
by the crickets and the stars . . .

13

(. . . *The water celebrates dawn* . . . Popular Ballad)

The moon was gilding the river,
—coolness of the break of day—
from the sea the waves were coming
tinted by the hues of dawn . . .

The weak, sad countryside
gradually received the light . . .
Came the cricket's broken song,
the hidden plaint of the well . . .

The wind fled to its cave,
horror went back to its den;
in the greenness of the pines
wings opened, one by one . . .

The stars now began to die,
the mountainside turned to rose;
yonder from the garden well
rose the swallow's morning song.

14

14

The path has fallen asleep;
tonight no one will return . . .
The gilded moon watches over
the sadness of the valley.

I looked out the garden grille
and saw a man turn away . . .
He turned to look back; he had
a very menacing look.

I offered him bread . . . He would
not take it, nor say "God bless you."
I said to him, "Go with God . . ."
He went away without answering.

Last night I looked out my window
to see the moon. It was late . . .
I saw a shadow in my garden . . .
A dog was barking . . . It was

someone walking in the garden . . .
The night was not angel-watched . . .
A rook was cawing now far . . .
now near . . . moving through the trees . . .

I offered him bread . . . He would
not take it, nor say "God bless you . . ."
The path has fallen asleep;
tonight no one else will pass . . .

15

A good evening to you, village.
I am Juan, your homesick son.
I have come to see how spring
is flowering in your fields.

Do you remember me? I
am Blanca's lover, the pale
poet who deserted you
one morning in May.

And I carry in my heart
a treasure that I have found
hidden in the fragrant roses
of the romanticists' garden.

Sun-filled village, shall I speak
to you my old languid feelings?
or do you want April songs
filled with sunshine and birds?

Tell me now; and I will open
my heart to you, and my lips,
and there will fly over you
a covey of canticles!

A good evening to you, village.
I am Juan, your homesick son.
Give me with your happy sunshine
a kiss, full upon my lips.

16

Pomegranates against blue sky!
street of the mariners!
how very green are your trees!
how laughing is your sky!

Capricious wind from the sea!
street of the mariners!
eye of grey, golden forelock
dusky, florid, wind-tanned face.

The wife sings in the doorway:
"What a life the sailors lead!
the man always gone to sea,
one's heart always in the wind!"

—Virgin of Carmen, may
your hands always guide the oars,
beneath your eyes may the sea
be mild and the sky be blue!

At late afternoon the air
glimmers, the west is all dreams;
it is the gold of yearning,
of mourning and memories . . .

Capricious wind from the sea!
street of the mariners!
blue sailor's blouse, and the wonder-
working Virgin wrought upon it.

Pomegranates against blue sky!
street of the mariners!
the man always gone to sea,
and one's heart riding the wind!

In the distance come the ox-carts . . .
the pine grove and wind have said it,
the golden moon has announced it,
the smoke and echo repeat it.

The ox-carts going by
these afternoons after sunset,
are the ox-carts that are taking
the dead tree trunks from the woods . . .

How the passing ox-carts weep
on the road to Pueblo Nuevo!

The oxen dream as they come
under the light of the stars;
they dream of the warm stable
smelling of milk and hay.

And behind the slow ox-carts
slowly the drivers walk,
with the goad upon their shoulders
and their eyes on the sky.

How the passing ox-carts weep
on the road to Pueblo Nuevo!

In the peace of countryside
the dead tree trunks leave behind
a fresh and honest aroma
of their wide-open heart.

From the tower of the old town
the Angelus' benediction
floats above the new-turned fields
with their cemetery fragrance.

How the passing ox-carts weep
on the road to Pueblo Nuevo!

When the ox-carts go by
the gate leading to my orchard,
I recite for the poor trunks
a faltering Pater Noster;

and I imagine a shower
of roses for the old trees
to give comfort to the nests
on these winter afternoons.

How the passing ox-carts weep
on the road to Pueblo Nuevo!

18

White donkey; yellow and green
of the autumn grapevines;
old, white donkey, your mourning
is ornamented with grief.

You are gold in the late sun,
and the leaves of greenish gold
are lighted up, as in a
springtime filled with sobbing.

And the blue afternoon holds,
when you pass, a melancholy
brightness of elegy, sun
in the crystal of your eyes!

White donkey; yellow and green
of the autumn grapevines;
who has burdened your old
age with the sad treasure?

You remember . . . white butterflies
used to play above the brook;
there were yellow lilies
under a sky blue and gold;

the meadow was filled with rain
and you gazed there as though
it were meadow of pearls . . .
—the air turns odorous—

White donkey; yellow and green
of the autumn grapevines;
gentle white donkey, your mourning
is ornamented with grief!

19

The sunlight will gild the leaves,
will give diamonds to the river,
make a song of gold and laughter
with the wind, through the pines.

With their lips filled with roses,
children will come to the garden,
broken the gold of their dreams
or holy virgins and lilies . . .

He who carries the sad news
along the dust of the road
will see white butterflies
and crystal drops of dew.

"Good morning." "Good day to you."

Light-hearted town full of flowers,
you will gradually be filled
with sun, white smoke, blue smoke,
with bells and idyllic songs.

. . . And then, when the noonday comes,
there will be peace . . . Among
the pine trees a bird will sing . . .
and all will be mute and sere.

20

This is the village. Above
the darkening rooftops, green
and weeping with the sheep bells
and with crickets, lie the fields.

This is the hour of bats,
when the angel rings Angelus,
when the laborer comes home,
with his hoe, singing a song.

And there is cry of children,
there is lowing in the stable,
a warm odor of the hearth,
and smoke in blue and white!

And there a golden moon
that, from the distant pine groves,
tinges with crystal light
the deserted countryside.

21

Gladden, gladden, puppet-player,
with your drum the night hour . . .
　　　the path
has its branches all in flower.

The moon from behind the hill,
has shown its dead face before . . .
　　　the cabin
has already closed its door.

In the valley Aurora sleeps;
night wanders down from the hill;
　　　in the distance
weeps the sad heart of the mill.

Green meadows and lovely nights,
lovely for weeping and flight!
　　　the stars
tremble, tremble in the sky.

Gladden, gladden, puppet-player,
with your drum the night hour . . .
　　　the path
has its branches all in flower.

Garden, heart without a name,
ancient piece of mended silk,
　　　woman, man,
humpback, and a rosy limb,

kiss that is painted in red . . .
just the pantomime of love!
　　　the eye laughs
over hunger, over pain.

Perhaps the crowd does not care
for so much passionate bent . . .

in the town
what know they of sentiment!

Gladden, gladden, puppet-player,
with your drum the night hour . . .
the path
has its branches all in flower!

The children and women are
breezes and roses; afar,
moon, you are
of all things the arbiter!

Sancho, the priest and the barber,
will always disapprove; sad
but
the pathway is for the mad . . .

And if by chance they should halt
all tired out with misfortune,
they will leap
and go to sleep in the moon!

Gladden, puppet-player, gladden
with your drum the night hour . . .
the path
has its branches all in flower!

OLVIDANZAS (1906–1907)

22

We thought that everything was
broken, ruined, and stained . . .
—But, within, reality
smiled, and waited for us.

Tears, blood-stained and warm
against the frost-covered panes . . .
—But, inside, reality
smiled, and waited for us.

The black day was close to ending,
muddled in dank misery . . .
—But, inside, reality
smiling, awaited us—

23

I fired at the ideal,
thinking that I would not hit.
—Black shot, how your recoil
shattered my soul!

The evening, after the shot
that split its very being,
hushed, of a sudden, turned
dark green, its forehead pallid.

And I heard, deep in my heart,
that, throbbing, awaited it,
the abrupt thud of the dead
sky, with its folded wings.

BALADAS DE PRIMAVERA (1907)

24
Morning of the Cross

God is bright blue. Now the flute and the drum
announce the coming of the cross of spring.
Long live the roses, the roses of love,
flecked with the sunlight of the meadow's green.

Come away to the green fields for rosemary,
come away, come away,
for rosemary and for love.

I said to her: "And will you let me love you?"
She answered me, radiant with youthful love:
"The day the cross of spring is in full bloom,
I will love you with all my heart and soul."

Come away to the green fields for rosemary,
come away, come away,
for rosemary and for love.

"The cross of spring is in full bloom, my love.
Love, the cross, love, now is at its height!"
She answered me, "And now you want my love?"
And the morning pierced me with its light!

Come away to the green fields for rosemary,
come away, come away,
for rosemary and for love.

The drum and flute enliven our rejoicing.
The butterfly is here with fancy's part.
My sweetheart is the virgin of the garden,
and she will love me now with all her heart.

Come away to the green fields for rosemary,
come away, come away,
for rosemary and for love.

25

Night Song

There goes the scent
of the rose!
   Seize it in your ecstasy!

There goes the light
of the moon!
   Seize it in your plenitude!

There goes the song
of the brook!
   Seize it in your liberty!

26

April
(The day and Robert Browning)

The blue titmouse in the poplar.
—And what else?
The poplar against blue sky.
—And what else?
The blue sky within the water.
—And what else?
Water in the small new leaf.
—And what else?
The new petal in the rose.
—And what else?
The new rose within my heart.
—And what else?
And my heart within your own!

27

Green Greenfinch

Green greenfinch,
sweeten the sunset hour!

Enchanted palace,
the pine grove at evening
sobs a lullaby
to the river's fleeing.
There the greenfinch
has his darkling nest.

Green greenfinch,
sweeten the sunset hour!

The last breeze of day
sighs heavily;

the red sun makes rainbows
on the weeping pine.
Our vague and languid
hour, greenfinch.

Green greenfinch,
sweeten the sunset hour!

Solitude and calm;
majesty and silence.
The hut of the soul
locks the door and prays.
Suddenly, O beauty!
the greenfinch sings.

Green greenfinch,
sweeten the sunset hour!

His song enraptures.
—Has the wind stopped?
The fields are imbued
with his loving plaint.
Mauve is his lament,
green the greenfinch.

Green greenfinch,
sweeten the sunset hour!

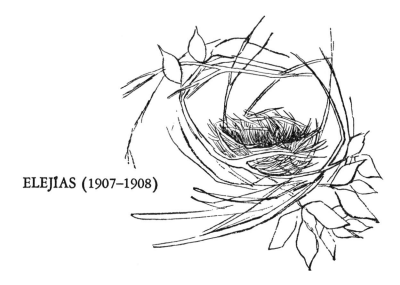

ELEJÍAS (1907–1908)

28

(. . . Et chaque feuille d'or tombe, à l'heure venue,
Ainsi qu'un souvenir, lente sur le gazon.
A. Samain)

One by one the dry leaves are falling
from my withered heart, yellowed and sorrowful.
The water that once gushed there in laughter
is motionless and black, without sky or song.

Was it a dream, my green tree, my crown of coolness,
my fountain in the roses, with sunshine and song?
Was that springtime but a season of sad madness?
Only wind that bright covey of illusions?

My trunk will dry up, with its deserted nest;
and the nightingale that was mirrored in the pool
will hush, cold spectre, on the motionless branch,
turned to ashes by the senescence of the moon.

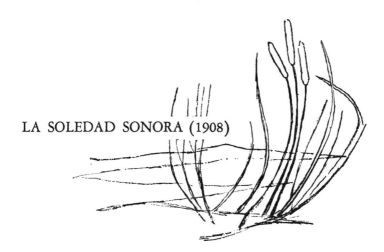

LA SOLEDAD SONORA (1908)

29

The wind has swept away the clouds of sadness;
the greenness of the garden is a fresh treasure;
the birds have returned in the path of beauty
and in the clear sunset blooms a garden of gold.

Inflame me, sunset! Make me perfume and flame;
let my heart be like you, sunset! Uncover in me
what is eternal, what burns and what loves,
. . . and let winds of oblivion bear away all grief.

30

Dried up, ruined fountain, you are now but a rock!
—O former voice of silver, O sweet and limpid font—
A greenfinch takes your grave for a well, and the clinging
ivy hangs upon you like an indolent maid.

Water palace abandoned by your wellspring, dried
as my life has dried, to safeguard your story;
but the evening sun dreams of what you left behind,
as a golden spray sings in my memory.

31

The crystal moon is moving, green, clear, and new,
like a demented queen among the white birch trees . . .
She smiles at me, bows, throws me a kiss, and takes
my heart away with her, rolling along blue skies!

She rocks it in her arms, garlands it with stars,
cradles it in a cloud, mirrors it in a stream . . .
brings it down to the roses, and, odorous from them,
indolently lays it down to sleep in empty space!

She imparts to it her warmth, her crystal and her gold,
and when at dawn she brings it back to my bleeding
    breast,
my poor heart is like a precious forlorn token,
starry, fragrant, wet, and heavy with sleep.

POEMAS MÁJICOS Y DOLIENTES (1909)

32
Winter Etching

(Snow)

Where have all the colors gone to hide
this black and white day?
the foliage, black; water, gray; the sky
and earth, of a pale black-and-white;
and the sorrowful town
an old etching of romantic times.

The passer-by, black;
black the faint-hearted bird
that flies across the garden like a dart . . .
Even the silence is faded and harsh.

Evening falls. The sky
has not a softness in it. A vague
yellow in the west is almost luminous,
almost not. Afar, the countryside
of arid iron.

And night comes on, as might
a funeral train; everything
in black and cold, no stars, but white
and black, like the black and white day.

ARTE MENOR (1909)

33

The Present

New gold
of the dawn;
old gold
of the sunset;
rival archers
of my panting
breast,
the old, the new!

34

Pre-Spring

It rains on the river . . .

The fragrant rushes
of green river edge
shiver in the rain . . .

what an anxious scent
of cold petals!

It rains on the river.

My boat seems to be
my dream, in a vague
dream world. O green shore!
O rudderless boat!
O cold heart!

It rains on the river . . .

POEMAS AGRESTES (1910–1911)

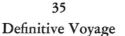

35
Definitive Voyage

... And I shall go. And the birds will go on singing;
and my garden will remain here, with its green tree,
and its white well.

Each afternoon the sky will be blue and calm;
and the bells in the bell tower will ring
just as this evening they are ringing.

And they will die, those who have loved me;
the village will be new each year;
and in that nook of my whitewashed, flowering garden,
my homesick spirit will wander.

And I shall go; and I shall be alone, homeless, with no
green tree, no white well,
without a blue and placid sky ...
And the birds will go on singing.

36

New Leaves

(To Isoldita Esplá)

See how the golden children climb
up to the sky through the silver poplars!
With eyes uplifted to the sky,
the blue, they climb, like simple dreams.
See how the golden children climb
up to the sky through the silver poplars.

And the blue of their beautiful
eyes and the sky touch . . . They are one, eyes and sky!
See how the golden children climb
up to the sky through the silver poplars!

37

I walked into the shrub.
Oh how it smelled,
how it smelled of life!

I walked into the stream.
Oh how it fled,
how it fled toward life!

LABERINTO (1910–1911)

38

In the town of stone, rain-drenched and solitary,
the evening moon rises, like a climbing rose;
there are regal gardens that hold it for an instant
softly gilded among their broad full leaves . . .

Along the river, serpent between thick blackened
      walls,
it makes a golden bubbling, tremulous in the shade;
kindles the sentinel's rough bugle, it is watched
from the prisons, through sordid windowpanes . . .

It drops like rain a dream of peace and tenderness
over the coming thought . . . and on the gloomy walls
paints mauve landscapes and distant villages
with melancholy flowers and melancholy bells . . .

MELANCOLÍA (1910–1911)

39

(Moguer)

Nightfall. Large clouds smother the town.
The street lamps stand, drowsy and sorrowful,
and the yellow moon travels between rain and wind.

A moist odor ascends from the countryside.
A star rises, greenish by the old spire.
The seven-o'clock stagecoach goes by . . . Dogs bark . . .

Coming out on the road, one feels upon his face
the cold moonlight . . . From the white cemetery
upon the hill, comes the sobbing of the tall black pines.

POEMAS IMPERSONALES (1911)

40

To the Moon of Art

*(... After having so well served
the crown of his true king ...*
                        J. D. Manrique
Sun of the sleepless!
                        Lord Byron)

I gave you, sleepless sun, one heartbeat at a time,
every bit of my heart. Your luminous crown
as faithful, noble liege, I have faithfully served.
I no longer have arms to offer you, nor town.

You, on the other hand, rewarding fealty,
which neither thralls nor saddens nor degrades,
have granted me, O queen, the divine attribute
of having, as you have, a restless soul awake.

45

When death finally comes to knock upon my door,
he will find in my hut a log among dead leaves.
Yes, my fragrance already perfumes your garden's blue.
My song is now eternal nightingale of your dream!

41

To a Poet
for an Unwritten Book

Let us create the names.
They will determine men.
Then, they will determine things.
And there will remain only the world of names,
words of the love of men,
of the fragrance of roses.

Of love and roses
there will persist only the names.
Let us create names!

42
Echo

    I was sad, and I howled
to the summer fields in rage.
My voice, against the burning reddish rock
that resembled an open heart exposed,
resounded through the fearful labyrinths
of an unknown echo. And the rock,
come alive at my cry, became
a great frenetic face,
that looked at me in glee, listened
in glee, and answered me
in glee, in terrifying glee.

43

Annunciation

Vision in crystal
lovely as a Damascene art work!

From the slight corridor
a simple view,
the garden. And Mary,
virgin, timid, full
of grace, head bowed like a lily's,
submissive to the heavenly message.

A vivid little bird
fluttered above a rose.
Dawn was fair in repose.
And like the moon at dawn,
Gabriel's wing, triumphant and white,
vanished in the innocent new sun.
Memory crystal-bright!

APARTAMIENTO (1911–1912)

44

Neighborhood Park
(Love, a lion
that feeds on human hearts)

—Ring of little girls. Fragile, white
choir of silver-threaded singing,
though still the sun with red-gold light
adorns the greenness of the evening:

(Love, a lion
that feeds on human hearts.)

How you remain poised on the sunset,
quivering voices, dagger thrusts
of innocence! And how your song
breaks in foretaste of suffering!

... Love, a lion
that feeds on human hearts.

—Eyes in the circle, flower of mourning
among the tree trunks. Lovely voices
—beside the fountain—that in the sky
show through like stars:

> *Love, a lion*
> *that feeds on human hearts—*

Do no thinking. Laugh at the weeping
song! Nothing is worth your misery!
. . . You will weep later, when a future
hour brings back this memory.

> . . . Love, a lion
> that feeds on human hearts.

Evenings will come in which the past,
in such another touching choir,
will bring this sunset, purple then,
back to the truth of daily life.

> *Love, a lion*
> *that feeds on human hearts—*

Leap now and laugh; there is not yet
pall of mourning to mute this laughter!
. . . Some day you'll die for love, oh yes!
Oh yes, some day you will break hearts!

> . . . Love, a lion
> that feeds on human hearts.

45

Remembrance goes
along my memory, pushing aside
with subtle feet the withered leaves.

—Behind, the house is empty.
In front, highways
leading somewhere else, deserted,
rigid.
And the rain weeping there by the eyeful,
as if the eternal hour had been blinded—

Though the house is mute and shuttered,
though I am not there, I am there.
And . . . Good-bye, you who are walking away
without once looking back!

46
They

All things for them, all, all:
vineyards, beehives, pine groves, wheat fields . . .

—I have had
enough
with my daydream of light,
my divine inspiration.

I have been like the rose, wholly perfume;
just like the water, constant restlessness;
and they were firm earth to my eager root
and human river bed for my proud flood—

. . . All; for if they have never thought,
what paupers have they been!

LA FRENTE PENSATIVA (1911–1912)

47

Who can know the reverse of any hour?
How often has the dawn
been behind a hill!
How often the horizon's regal splendor
held thunder in its golden heart!
A certain rose was poison.
A deadly sword gave life.
I imagined a flower-filled
green meadow at the ending of a road,
and I found a morass.
I dreamed of glory in humankind,
and found divinity.

48

Winter Song

Singing. Singing.
Where are the singing birds singing?

It has rained. The branches
are still leafless. They sing. The birds
sing. Where are the singing
birds singing?

I have no birds in cages.
There are no boys who sell them. They are
singing. The valley is far away. Nothing . . .

I do not know where they are
singing, the birds, singing, singing,
the birds that are singing.

49

O painter who painted me
in this vague tableau of life
so well, that I almost seem
to be real; Oh paint me
again, and badly, so that I
may seem unreal.

PUREZA (1912)

50

(Autumn)

Still the crescent moon
shines red among the pines.
—A silent band of starlings passes by—
From the walled orchard crystal-bright
with the dew turned to frost,
a raucous blackbird whistles,
and, clean, the open roads
march eastward.

All things take fire from the white and red
hard flame of dawn's bright sweep . . .
—The guiltless brow laughs against the sky;
and black-faced guilt, a coward, bends to weep.

. . . O sweet cold thrill!
How from the happy heart and from the grove
the dew falls silently
like a liquid dream of silk and gold!

Mild dawning of a Christmas-seeming day,
giving the cold perfume of rosemary;
across your infinite, sudden fire
the soul takes flight!
                    The flesh
is left, a pile of rottenness,
like a dead mule, in the path's mortuary.

51

Cold is the night and pure.

The clean-faced moon obliquely
whitens the wall.
          Dark
and round, the scarlet sage, waving
its chalices drenched with heavy dew,
perfumes the calm.
          A weeping star
is turning toward the west,
a green-hued trembling above the single locust tree . . .

The earth spins audibly.
          And in the hour,
clear and full of grace,
humility attains
eternal beauty: the peaceful, silver
donkey that calls, in high decree,
to absent brother; the breeze,
forgetful of the poor and well-known beach;
the tardy cricket; the watchful rooster
awakening one moment
the roses with his voice that breaks up whitenesses
along the plains of dawn . . .
          Bethlehem comes
to all the barnyards . . .

Almost colorless, the colors
seem made of glass.

52

The lamb baaed gently.
The tender donkey showed its joy
in lusty bray.
The dog barked playfully
almost talking to the stars.

I could not sleep. I went outdoors
and saw heavenly tracks upon the ground
all flower-decked
like a sky
turned upside down.

A warm and fragrant mist
hovered over the grove;
the moon was sinking low
in a soft golden west
of divine orbit.

My breast beat without pause,
as if my heart had wined . . .

I opened wide the stable door to see
if He were there.
                    He was!

SONETOS ESPIRITUALES (1914–1915)

53

To the Sonnet with My Soul

As in the wing infinite flight exists,
and in the flower the wandering perfume,
in the flame the moving lucent bloom,
and in the blue the only sky persists;

as in a song is comfort for grief's spell,
in water's flow, coolness that vivifies,
and noble richness in the diamond's guise,
so in my flesh does total longing dwell.

In you, O sonnet, this pure yearning finds
its image, as within a quiet pool,
reflected its immortal miracles.

The unending clarity of its beauty shines
like the sky of a fountain, limitless
within the limits that your shores impose.

54

Brief Return

What was she like, dear God, what was she like?
O my deceitful heart, uncertain mind!
Was she the passing of a gentle wind?
Or like the springtime's swift and sudden flight?

So slight she was, so voluble, so light,
like summer thistle down . . . Yes! undefined
like a smile lost in laughter, unconfined
and vain in air, a waving banner bright!

Banner, smile, or thistle down, a winged
June springtime, purely breeze, no less!
How frantic was your carnival, how poor!

All your changefulness became no thing
—remembrance, blind bee of bitterness—
I never knew just what you really were!

55

The Broken Heart

I had believed that my poor heart had been
completely mended. I had tied it with
the strings of poetry, my lyric withe
in its high purity.

My green
new springtime was beginning to send forth
fresh blossoms as I passed; and dreams of peace
and songs of gladness brought a new surcease
with the sunlight into my bit of earth.

Suddenly, among the roses, you appeared,
full of laughter as always, changeable
as always, leaping nets and setting snares . . .

My noble gaze at once became austere,
and my badly tied heart, unchangeable,
fell in pieces once more, unprepared.

56
October

I lay upon the earth, my eyes upon
the infinite fields of old Castile
which autumn wrapped in softness to reveal
the clear bright yellow of its setting sun.

The slow plow had in parallel begun
to open up the dark soil and unseal
in honesty the womb in which the seed
the simple open hand dropped one by one.

I thought of pulling out my heart and throwing
it with all its exalted sympathy
into the furrow of the tender earth,

to see if by this breaking and this sowing
the spring would have to show the world a tree
to which eternal love had given birth.

57

Travesty

I never thought the snow-white lily could
be fetid iris too. I did not know
that hatred could nourish gayety.
O winter, you have been called early spring!

Why should the haughty and unsullied star
be a dry cradle of the shadowy night?
How could the immortal dove of peace incite
the crooked beak of the flesh-eating hawk?

Yet the life-giving spring with its black spray
has veiled in mourning morning's aureole.
The nightingale could a man's fears inflame.

The child spoke with words impure,
the heart was only an unhealthy hole,
and treachery has borne a stainless name.

58

Ideal Nights

(Under the acacia in bloom)

Beneath the divine light of heaven's stars
that look down on my infinite distress,
my eyes roam through the heavens, comfortless,
insanely lost among the stars.

These clear-eyed stars are those that long ago
on guiltless nights of passion and of yearning,
came down, turned into hands, to earth
to play with my fair joys below.

O climbing, O descent of pain and grace,
eternal correspondence of ideal
cares, ever vainly satisfied!

Wrapped in the aroma of the acacia's breath
like two immortal children side by side
play human heaven and the heavenly mind.

59

Spring

(To a woman)

The rose exhales its most divine bouquet,
the star is shining with its purest light,
the nightingale embraces the delight
of the night in its deepest roundelay.

And the sweet odor sickens me, the ray,
of brilliant blue, leaves a gloomy blight
upon me, while the night bird's crystal flight
of song, makes me sob, dejection's prey.

And this is not that enormous despair
that used to lick my former ancient heart
with its honeyed, insuperable tongue . . .

Let the scent of the rose be placid, fair,
the star inflame me with the poet's art,
let me delight in the nightingale's song!

60
Love...!

From so much walking on the bitter hills
of my existence, wearisome and slow,
my naked, bleeding feet no longer know
pleasure in paths where fragrant flowers spill.

How finely matched are these two combatants,
the foot that conquers and the intellect!
The stout heart, with what contentment decked,
thinks of May, budding in sufferance!

It's autumn now, and in the pure and stark
path of my life, where fragrance is unknown,
the drying leaves have turned my head to gold . . .

Love! Love! April is turning dark!
Summer's abundance I no longer grasp!
I even find divine my dismal woe!

61
King of Vanities

The evening crowned by doleful discontent
with its multiple beams of radiance,
and these sere flowers were magnificence
of gold, around my head vile ornament.

From the high peak of sovereign command,
I smiled, victorious, at my woeful plaints;
I savored as if honey grief and pain,
and believed beauty lay in sorrow's pang.

Being a woman, evening, proud and vain,
shed her garments of light, and things were shorn
of all desire, wrapped in senselessness . . .

I was myself once more. My wreath of frayed
flowers became gold butterflies air-borne,
and I became king of forgetfulness.

62

Man Alone

Gay and miraculous self-mastery
that liberates! . . . I went off singing,
to the green countryside. The sky was soft,
the brook lively, the wind gamboling free.

Pure as a child again, my thoughts
strayed from me to their inmost depths
hiding from my unknown heart. And walking,
walking, I felt a new and fresh insight.

With what delight I followed butterflies,
how I plucked mallows growing by the hedge,
how with my hand I choked the fountainhead!

Lost in the dawn of all things,
I was the universe, reborn, full-fledged,
out of the heart of the old trunk long dead.

63

The Garden

It was—No, not thus,—but otherwise.
The springtime still in green was not
the glory of the sun, but seemed somewhat
to be, yet it was not . . . yes, in this guise!

Today, upon the bench that springtime
hangs with green and keeps from harmony,
it seems as though the winter's villainy
turns cold and deep the ardent burgeoning.

No, this is not the place. There is no scope
for yearning here, but timeliness, and none
are troubled or in fear of destined change.

It is April, for this is April's range,
but it is not, for in its greening dawn
there is no rising of my sun of hope!

64

Hope

To hope! To hope! Meanwhile the sky festoons
with brilliant clouds of gold the clouds of rain;
the ripened spikes succeed the roses' reign;
the withered leaves the spikes; the ice too soon

buries the leaf; the nightingale, undone,
bemoans the flight of nights of love, the pain
of parting; and the butterflies amain
double their flight in the warmth of the sun.

Now in the glow of rustic candlelight,
the lowly cradle of my dreams is swayed
by garish winds of red October's blast ...

My flesh turns more divine,
timeworn, old, my illusions now are gray,
and what I hope for is, alas, my past.

65
Elegy

My boredom is repeated in the stream,
slow and silent, like another god
among the golden poplars that are sending
a song up to the free and limpid sky.

My life is but this double burning scene:
my feet beside my feet, interlacing
their roots; and my brow separating
in immense rift my mind from its desire.

All human autumn freely leans
toward this last and glowing evening hour,
as to a soft and life-throbbing cote;

where from the reflections in the stream
my daydreams overturned, I see my life
more beautiful than dreams, and more remote.

66

Autumn

October at the bland and gentle blowing
of south wind scatters golden leaves and red,
and at the limpid falling of the leaves
carries our thoughts toward the infinite.

What grateful peace in this withdrawal
of everything, O meadow dropping old
petals, and rain already cold,
moistening the wind with trembling crystal drops!

Bewitchery of gold! Captivity
in which the body, become soul, dissolves
in tenderness, on a green hill supine!

In the presence of beauty's bright decay,
life sheds her garments, and in light resolves
the loftiness of her own truth divine.

ESTÍO (1915)

67
You

All others pass by, green, red . . .
You are up above, all white.

All the others, rowdy, rough . . .
You are above, unperturbed.

They pass by, deceitful, lewd . . .
You are above, modest, chaste.

68

Like the breeze, you remind us
of wind;
the sea you recall, like the brook;
as life does, you bring heaven
to mind;
and like death, you remind us
of earth.

69

The shadow, it seems,
brings you nearer . . .
Come through the tunnel
of enfolding dark!
I await you, hidden . . .
You will be unseen . . .

The silence, it seems,
brings you nearer . . .
I come in the cloak
of hushed solitude!
Wait for me in silence . . .
I shall be unheard . . .

Silent and concealed
—none will ever know—
in silence and darkness
the immortal haunt,
from love we will fashion
voice and shining light.

70

How can I place in time
the vague feeling of you?

Toward the dawn! Too much!
Toward the sunset! Less!

It falls a little short
or long, by finger's breadth . . .

—Your laughter rings, fine-spun,
close to me . . . from afar—

71

Like an immaculate sword,
let written reflection give
to the infinite day's sun
virtue of its lambent flame.

—Light comes flashing, to and fro,
beginning at its small haft,
from the east down to the west,
of its immaculate sky.

Just like a sword, let all thought
turn within itself, its core,
and remain all in itself
as steel within the sword.

72

(*You hold my heart.*
Camõens)

Suddenly, a strange emptiness,
anxiety without cause . . .
—My heart!
And placing my hand
on my pain, I hesitate,
I do not know, do not know
what has become of my heart!

My heart! The whole world in it
painlessly found room one day.
Or it would leave me for heaven
without deserting its cell.
I do not feel its old weight,
it is not above, and I
no longer have it! No more
shall I count upon its treasures
in my oblivion! No, no longer
can I find—clear days—
beauty, love, glory, and God.

Suddenly, a strange emptiness,
anxiety without cause.

73

When she has gone away
is when I see her clear.
Then when she has returned,
she disappears.

76

74

Now is when I have committed
all those ancient wretched things;
is when their dry leprosy
blackens me and makes me bleed.

—Clear days that held within
already the deep promise
of this truth, how could you keep
concealed this festering wound?

—The sky has become all soiled
suddenly; like blinded,
evil clouds, all my forgotten
bygone springs pass before me—

Now is when I have committed
all those ancient wretched things,
now that they have, chosen woman,
made you weep with pain and grief.

75

Faster, earth, faster;
faster, faster, sun;
set at odds the system,
for love awaits me now.

What matter if the universe
be upset, earth, sun?
All is smoke; the only joy:
that love awaits me now.

Let snow take the wheat!
Hurry, earth! Fly, sun!
Shorten my season of hoping,
for love awaits me now!

76

How does an outer voice
come to be our voice
and cause our heart to speak
its thinking and its words?

77

Days, days, days, days!
But the one day never comes.
April, an imagined chrome,
not April part of spring.
The will smiles to itself
Underfoot the earth is weeping.

In the middle, evening. Vivid
gold burnishes the grove
and around it, life is the
fire that enkindles it;
the bird sings in laughter
its crystal promise to love;
the blooming flower's fragrance
reaches the senses through the flesh.

Every hilltop displays
open plains with lonely moon.
The bird that sang close at hand
always sings in other boughs.
Nights, nights, nights, nights!
But the one night never comes.

78

Is the body hungrier
or the soul? And for what? If I
please the body, then the soul
is the one that yearns . . . for what?
If, sated, I feed the soul,
then the body longs . . . for what?
The body sated, the soul
is gold; if the soul, it is
the body that turns to gold.

Love of body and of soul!
When, oh when, will the day come,
the eternal honeymoon
of these two enamoured ones?

79

You Are Not

You are not.

(Hands always upon the heart.
Silences in nook apart.
Absences from balcony . . .)

— . . . You are not.

(Little flirting glances stressed.
Impetuous interest.
Touching feet and fingers pressed . . .)

— . . . You are not.

(Like the wind, to sigh and sigh.
Like the rain, to cry and cry.
To sob and sob, like the sea . . .)

—You are not.

80
Yes!

(Solitary noon)

I left the yes to be interred
naked, so that it would be
always, always burrowing
upward, up!
from the earth possessed by death.

Yes! Always yes! Always watchful!
Piercing stem that displaces
all the rocks and opens then
its golden, permanent tongue
in the perennial bonfires
of the past,
of the present,
of the future . . .
　　　　　　Always.

81

(Yesterday, only, or tomorrow!
J. R. J.)

In the blue wind the verses
written this morning take flight . . .
Where are they,
the verses written today?

I have whatever I give
and only the present serves;
today is now
and only the present serves;
and love turns back at the scent
of pink, acacia, and jasmine,
at the scent
of pink, acacia, and jasmine.

Good resolutions . . . What for?
Let all things remain the same.
Faith and more faith.
Let all things remain the same!

August Daybreak

Sunrises of new dawns against the ancient walls
of cities that exist, yet we shall see no more!

Illness that once again after gaining strength
returns to the road, never to reach its end!

Morning of heavy storm, with a vast rainbow arched
above the wakened end of the sleep-silenced town!

*—It is known that the far away dear living ones
are away; and that the dear dead departed are dead—*

Railway trains that go by under the red-brick sun,
their dust-covered weariness dazzled by blood!

*—That what is done is done forever and forever,
that one can only weep, for nothing can be changed—*

Morasses that reflect the crimson of the dawn
to impossible ending in the drying marsh bed!

Mansions that yesterday left open, smothered
with roses, aflame in early-morning gold!

*—And innocence awakes in shabby disarray,
a bad taste in the mouth that yesterday kissed breeze . . .*

Loves that have been and are, that dawn renders
            unsure!
And passionate kisses that at dawn turn to naught!

Fields in which formerly a woman loved a man;
            sad pines,
sad paths, sad plains, sad hillocks.

. . . Eternal daybreak of cold and of distress,
depressing emergence from the cavern of sleep!

83

White at first, the full white
of innocence, blinding, white,
white of ignorance, white.

Then poison shimmers in green;
the body opens its windows;
and the white turns to black.

Battle between nights and days!
The wind murders the breeze,
the breeze the wind . . .
                              And the breeze
brings back the all-white, attained;
veritable white, white,
of eternity, white, white. . .

84

I set my heart ahead
toward the tranquil hour
as if it were a watch . . .

But happiness did not come
—happiness was at its post
and that trick was foolishness—
it never was the right time!

—Reality, all confused,
was living in the past hour
of that hopelessness—

With what grieving I turned back
your hour, joyless heart!

85

For one moment of delight
my soul held a rose in thrall;
but when I removed my soul
like a butterfly, it took flight.

86

I should like to impale you, hour,
as I might a butterfly,
on her heart.

        Your golden dreams
might flutter—one day at least—
over her ice-cold and headstrong
blood . . .

Where will you go, brief moment
of mine, butterfly uncaught?

87

With all the beloved hearts,
now buried, that once loved me,
cold, among dark, anguished griefs,
I feel myself partly buried.

With all the glorious hearts,
in glory now, that once loved me,
burning in gold, I feel now
myself a little transfigured.

88

I do not know how to leap
from the shore of today
to the shore of tomorrow.

The river carries, meanwhile,
the reality of this evening
to forlorn and hopeless seas.

I look to the east, the west,
I look to the south, the north . . .
All the golden truth that once
used to encircle my soul,
as with a total sky,
now falls down, shattered and false.

. . . And I do not know how to leap
from the shore of today
to the shore of tomorrow.

89

How gay it is, in spring,
to watch the winter shed
its garments from its flesh,
leaving it in ephemeral
fellowship with the roses
also of tender flesh!

Now, in autumn, how sweet
it is to watch the flesh
of summer, quietly,
drop from the spirit, giving in friendliness
dried spiritual leaves!

90
Convalescence

Only you are with me, friendly sun.
Like a watchdog of light, you lick my white bed;
and I lose my hand in your golden hair,
my tired, strengthless hand.

How much of what has been
goes away . . . farther still!
                          Silent
I smile like a child,
and let you lick me, gentle sun.

. . . Suddenly, sun, you spring erect,
true guardian of my ruin,
and in feverish mad clamor
you bark at the vain phantoms
that, mute shadows, threaten
me from the sunset of the desert.

91

I shall dig from the dawn.
When the sun is in the west,
facing the west, dawn for me
will be its exaltation.

I shall dig the hardened rock
until the one bloom apart
that heaven draws from the clay
will touch me within my heart.

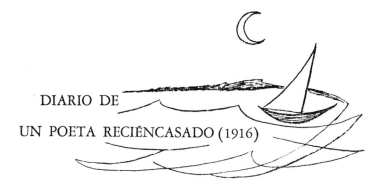

DIARIO DE
UN POETA RECIÉNCASADO (1916)

92

Madrid
January 17, 1916

> How close now to the soul
> what is still so immensely far away
> from one's hands!
>
> Like the light of a star,
> like a voice without name
> brought by sleep, like the trot
> of a faraway horse
> that we hear, anxiously,
> with ear to the ground;
> like the sea in telephone . . .
>
> And life is lived within,
> with the unquenchable light
> of a day of delight
> that shines somewhere else.
>
> Oh how sweet, what a sweet
> truth without reality as yet, how sweet!

93

Madrid,
January 17.

Roots and wings. But let the wings grow roots
and the roots fly.

94

At Moguer
January 21

First almond tree in bloom,   (aloud)
tender whiteness so chaste,
how well you come to meet me
the way her soul would come!   (low)
—...her soul, that last night came,
along La Mancha way,
watching my wakefulness
with her white beauty,
upon the fallen cloud,   (no longer spoken)
in the swift-falling rain
in the swirls of smoke,
in the moonlight that fell
on my soul . . .

95

From San Juan to Moguer, by stagecoach
January 21

Grace

(To You)

This grace with neither first nor last name
is the one you have.
                    The jumble
of heavenly blue and gold of your laughter,
your eyes, your hair,
are the blond beauty
of this tangle of clear sky and laughing sun
that pierces everything
with its singular grace.

Grace, divine tangle
without outlet or end; light,
grace, of color; grace, joy
of the light; color, grace,
of happiness!

96

Moguer,
January 25

Evening Nowhere

(Inner Sea)

. . . This instant
of peace—shadow awake—
in which the soul is sinking
down to the nadir of its vaulted sky!

This happy instant, without new delight,
like a golden lake
circled with misery!
— . . . The soul floods everything,
and remains
on high, alone,
outside—

This instant, infinite—down-sky—
within a long and slow
wave of the heart—awakened
blood—and an ancient, forgotten,
and newly-seen star!

97

January 30

Sky

Sky, a word
the size of the sea
we are forgetting behind us.

February 1

Monotony

The sea with waves of zinc and swells
of lime, besieges us
with its immense desolation.

All is the same—to north,
to east, to south, to west, sky and sea—
gray and hard,
plain and white.

Never a greater yawn
has so opened the world!

The hours follow the same rule
as all the sea and all the sky,
gray and white, plain and hard;
each hour is a sea, and gray and dry,
and a sky, hard and white.

Impossible to leave this woebegone
castle of the spirit!
In no matter what direction—to the west,
the south, the east, the north—
a sea of zinc and chalk,
a sky, just like the sea, of chalk and zinc.
—Unexpendable treasures of sadness—
with neither sunrise nor sunset . . .

February 2

Awakening

—O tardy will!

I saw of you,
night, only your tresses.

Your broad shoulders
could not remain a single instant more;
white—like the ruins of the moon—
they were torn in my recurring dream,
to which you, tearfully,
would turn your tired eyes, wide open,
to say good-bye to me when it was dawn.

Now that you are nothing but
a closed grave, the darkened shell
of your clear deep shadow, how useless
my tardy awakening, pure night!

February 5

Sun in the Cabin

(Dressing, while, under a momentary sunbeam, the canaries of the Cuban woman and the barber sing a new tune.)

Love, crimson rose,
how you delayed your flowering!
The struggle has now healed you,
and you are invincible.

Sun and rain have vied in you
struggling in a sad
transposition of color . . .
O impossible days!
Nothing was, except for instants,
what it had always been.
Free, the soul was imprisoned.
—At times, the rainbow's arc
but briefly shone
like a supreme prelude . . .—

But your new bud, rose,
hesitated still.
You went through convalescence
of childhood ills.
You opened yellow petals
in your difficult
burgeoning . . . Grief,
useless river, how you flowed!

Today, love, facing
the sun, you compete
with it; there is no glow
to match your virgin light.
Love, youth alone!
Love, original force!
Love, hand disposed
to all difficult soaring!
Love, clear-sighted gaze,
will inexpressible!

101

February 5

Sea

Only one moment!
                Yes, sea, to be
like you, various each moment,
crowned by the skies in their forgetfulness;
strong sea, without lapses—
calm sea
—with icy heart and eternal soul—
sea, obstinate image of the present!

102

Sky

I had forgotten you,
sky, and you were only
a vague existence of light,
seen—without name—
by my indolent, weary eyes.
And you appeared, among the dull
and hopeless words of the traveler,
like recurring brief lagoons
in a waterscape seen in dreams.

Today I gazed at you lingeringly,
and you have risen high as your name.

103

February 8

Imitation Sea

Yes. La Mancha, as water.
Desert of liquid make-believe.
Yes, La Mancha, bored, stolid.

Mute, behind sad-faced Sancho,
black against the red sunset where rain still falls,
goes Don Quijote with the evening sun
back to his village slow-moving and hungry
along the sunset paths—

O sea, quicksilver minus glass;
sea, mirror stippled with nothingness!

104

Birkendene, Caldwell
February 20

      I stripped you of petals, like a rose,
to look at your soul,
and I did not see it.

                  Yet everything around
—horizons of the land and of the sea—
all things, far as the infinite,
brimmed over with an immense
sharp and vivid fragrance

105

New York
April 27

Song

      Only I live within
the bosom of the spring!
You who see her outside
what know you of her core?
—If you go out to meet her
my dream is not disturbed . . . —
    Only I live within
the bosom of the spring!

May 1

Mauve Butterfly

Already the snow has left open to the sun the dried leaves of last autumn, which it kept smooth and intact under its white cold, and they cover all the ground. The trees, still without buds and flowers, have, against the windy blue, changeable crowns of white clouds. A small mauve butterfly flits among the creaking trunks and flies away, almost before we can see it.

"Look!"

By the time you look, it is gone, leaving an immense desolation the size of a minute's hope, which filled the whole countryside, in all the solitary valley, that adds to the sun-dried odor of the forest a thin sunny odor, fresh and new.

107

Mauve Butterfly

—There it goes!
          —The new primrose!

   They all run at once, mute, blind,
reckless, not knowing what it was,
only that someone cried:
There goes the new springtide!

   And they all return sad,
walking backwards, smiling frontwards,
with arms outspread,
and open hands.

—What a pity! It was!
They all run
here and there, blind, mute,
reckless among the dead tree trunks,
over the old dry leaves,
only that someone cried:
—It was!

All winter creaks, exhaling
pungency of dried wood and open
earth.
Oh, oh, oh, oh!
They all look up
at the sky, opening
immensely wide their eyes,
forgetful of the evening.

And they fall at last, downcast,
like a dead weed
burnt up with eagerness. Beside their dream
the mauve butterfly has remained poised.

New York
May 26

To Miranda
in the Stadium

> *(Come unto these yellow sands,*
> *and then take hands!*
> Shakespeare)

Miranda, Miranda, Miranda
fair and sweet and golden,
oh, don't take off your pristine robe
don't return to basement's dark
this illusion of your beauty
that, since from your mind transmuted,
is your truth.
   —The clock alight
on its tower, risen beside
the stars, has been lost to sight—

... Do not go from the stage
back to the sad and yellow sand!

Since on this night you did succeed
in being luminous, indeed
moved my soul to divine heights,
let us feed the rose of night
we plucked, with rain heaven-born,
that it may never be a thorn.
Let us both go where your heavenly
voice has gone,
let not oblivion
come like day between this, our night,
and the night tomorrow brings,
and the night tomorrow brings!

Miranda, let us go where your voice
has died, for me, in the open sea
of the constellated night.
That immaculate moon still
can tell me what has become
of your voice . . .
                    Miranda, come,
hurry, Gladys, I mean, Miranda,
Miranda, Miranda, Miranda!
from this blue, unreal and cold,
to the true immortal gold!

109

New York
June 4

One Day's Absence

Now, to dream is to see you;
and then, instead of dreaming,
living is to see the gleaming
of your light, till dying day.

To see your light! Neither dream
nor daydream. But only love,
easier and better to hold
than either dream or daydream.

Let my fantasy die!
To touch, to smell, to taste,
to hear, to see, illum-
inate your truth with mine;

since with the hidden flow
of your secret smile
you have left me beguiled,
with second sight endowed.

What clear fields you water,
unswerving stream, today!
Now indeed does my way
follow the eternal plains!

110

Sun in the Stateroom

*(Thinking while I bathe, see-
ing, through the open porthole, the blue sea in sunlight,
and singing, then, all morning.)*

No more dreams; to think
and to fasten the dart,
firm and straight upon
the goal so sweet to pierce.

All is simple and good;
the cloud on which I doubted
of everything, today
faith turns into a stronghold.

No more now to build
with illusory paste.
Since I have achieved heaven,
I have only to live.

June 15

Wide-Awake Sea

Oh, how wide-awake you are, rich sea,
whenever I, moody, stale from night-watching,
come out to look at you;
when I, my eyes black-ringed and puffy,
come out to look at you, each dawn.

Your heart, free, unconfined,
as big as all of you,
has no need of repose;
nor because you disturb
the countless deep loud pulsing of your heart
do you fear death coming
from any horizon.

How you play with your strength,
that bears every color
of the hours! How gay and wild
you rise and gather, become measureless beauty,
your ardent and icy dynamism,
your iron made movement,
standing always on yourself, tree of waves,
and upholding in your waters the whole sky!

Strong sea, Oh sleepless sea,
eternal contemplator, tireless
and endless, of the high and lone spectacle
of the sun and stars, eternal sea!

June 16

We Three

The ship's pennant, white,
is always lost among the very stars.
The only ones awake
are the sky, sea, and I—each one immense
as are the other two—.
               We talk, slow,
of other things, serenely and at length,
through early morning . . .

The ship's pennant, white,
remains, sharp in the wind, among the very stars,
the selfsame stars, though now a few
are missing . . .
             The cock crows
on the prow, and all awaken . . .
The sky assembles
all its remaining stars, the sea
its treasures, I my infinite,
and we depart from the luminous day
and, silent and asleep,
come to life's day.

June 17

My Gold

(To Manuel Machado)

We are entering gold. A pure gold
passes through us, engulfs, kindles,
eternalizes us.

How happy now the soul,
because it burns again,
becomes the only essence,
transmuted into heaven!

. . . Upon the sea, more blue, the sun, more golden,
liberates our soul,
dilates the tranquil heart
wide as the plenitude of the uncreated.

Gold, gold, gold, gold, gold,
only gold and all gold, nothing but gold
of music and of light and happiness!

Oh, once more I am flame,
I am once again the living tongue!

June 19

Iberia

Golden Iberia that I glimpse now through the mist,
approaching, every moment redder still
—lions become earth—
facing the sunset sky from which we come!
My own Iberia, crowned with cumulus opal and mauve!
Iberia, from this
pure, serene wind that bears us along!
—Oh, how good, blessed God,
it is to have a heart!

Lions become earth!
Walls of dried earth,
foremost, standing guardians, with their cloak
of wrinkles, of the mother,
poor, earnest, wounded!
—Oh how good, how good
it is to have a heart!

No! You will begin, Spain,
to bring forth gradually, as now for my soul,
facing the sun that is to rise for you,
tomorrow, all your soul in bloom, ardent and young,
earth become lions,
and flames instead of walls!
—Oh, how gay, how good
it is to have a heart!

June 20
four o'clock in the morning

Now!

The moon, now run aground in day, still
dazzles
the night of the half-purple sea,
where, filled by the northwest wind,
purple sails have
in their merry swelling
the rosy tint of the dawn . . .
The lighthouse still, now silvery and small,
cries out, three times each time,
Land, land, land!

Land once again. The last,
the first, mine,
land!

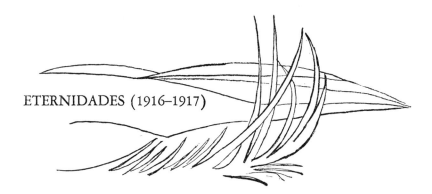

ETERNIDADES (1916–1917)

116
Action

Goethe

I have no words to say it,
for my speech
is not yet made.

117

Plentitude of today is
twig of tomorrow in bloom.
My soul must make the world over
in the image of my soul.

118

She first came to me pure,
arrayed in innocence.
I loved her as a child.

Then she began to dress
in outlandish robes.
Unwittingly, I began to hate her.

She came to be a queen,
ostentatious of riches.
What senseless wrath I felt, how full of gall!

. . . But she began disrobing.
And I smiled at her.

She left on only the tunic
of ancient innocence.
My trust in her returned.

And she removed the tunic,
and appeared wholly nude . . .
O passion of my life, Poetry,
naked, mine forever.

119

—Wait, light, wait!
—And I run, eager, wild—
Wait, light, wait!
—It waits, and when I go
to reach its side, it darkens,
cold.—
Wait, light, wait!
—And I drop to the ground, like a child,
weeping to myself, no longer seeing it:
wait . . . light . . . wait.—

120

To the ancient bridge of love,
old stone between high rocks
—date eternal, reddish dusk—
I have come bringing my heart:

—My only sweetheart is water
always flowing, not deceiving,
always flowing, never changing,
always flowing, never ending.

121

O time, tell me your secret
that makes you ever newer
the more you age!

Day after day, your past
is shorter, and your future greater,
—and your present
always the same as the one instant
when the almond tree blooms!

Time without trace:
tell me the secret of how every day
your spirit becomes one with your body!

122

Epitaph
of Me, Living

I died in sleep.
I rose again in life.

123

Life

What I believed locked to glory,
was the wide-open door
to this illumination.

Nameless domain!

Inexhaustible road
of successive gateways
leading always to reality!

Life without end!

124

How strange
we two with our instinct!

. . . Suddenly, we are four.

125

Night

The tree is flowering,
and the night takes away, each day,
half of its flowers.

—Oh, if it only counterfeited them
later, always, in the quiet water of its dream!

Life, semi-garden
of half-trees!

126

You are as beautiful
as the tender meadow under the rainbow
in the quiet noonday of rain and sun;
as the rippling curls of early spring
against the light of dawn;
as fine oats in stone-walled field
against the light of summer dusk;
as your green eyes beside my scarlet laughter,
and my deep heart with your vivid love.

127

I recognized you, for seeing the print
of your foot upon the path,
my heart that you trampled began to ache.

Madly I ran; I searched the livelong day,
like a masterless dog.

... You were already gone! And your feet ever fleeing
still trod upon my heart,
as though it were the road
that carried you forever ...

128

(Edgar A. Poe)

When you are lighted, beacon of my soul,
tower of dreams,
and you touch with your light the whole of life
—*this double silence, sea and shore*—
how beautiful you are!

Later, how sad
when your light is quenched,
beacon in daylight, tower of brick!

129

Clean I shall come
to you, as pebble in the brook,
laved in the torrent of my weeping.

Wait for me, clean
as the star after rain
—the rain of your tears—

130

I grasped the reins,
I turned the horse of dawn;
white,
I entered into life.

Oh, how they gazed at me,
frantic,
the flowers of my dream,
lifting up their arms to the moon!

131

My feet, how deeply sunk in earth!
My wings, how high up in the sky!
And what pain
in my heart pulled apart!

132

Forgers
of swords:
here is
the word!

133

Song

Once when your hands were moon,
they plucked your eyes, as divine
violets, from the garden of heaven.

How homesick now, your eyes,
remembering, at night, their mother-shrub
by the dead light of your hands!

All my soul, with its world,
I put in my earthborn eyes
to look at you, woman of light!

Will not your two violets
find fair the spot I show them,
finding the uncreated in my soul?

134

You stand before me, yes.
But I forget you,
thinking of you.

135

As long as you have left this one petal,
you are still a flower,
heart of mine.

—What dread! Pass quickly,
black early-morning gale!

136

Quiet Water

Love is, between you and me,
as impalpable, quiet, and complete,
as the invisible air,
the invisible water, between the moon
of the sky
and the moon in the river.

137

Like pebble in a well,
so lies my heart, with just the sky
above it and beneath it!

138

Perfectly though my soul
fits in my body—as
a single idea
within its perfect line—
yet will it have to go and leave
the body—like a grammarian's verse—
vain and stiff.

139

Yes, thirst, thirst, horrible thirst!
... But ... leave the water glass
empty! ...

140

Let your kisses flow
—just as a spring might flow—
a cool thread in the basin
of my heart!

My heart, later, in dreams
will return, double measure, the water of your kiss,
along the course of sleep, down
under life.

The water of your kiss
—O new dawn of the fountain—
will be eternal, eternal
for its spring will be my love.

141

Hush now! Savor the zenith,
listen to the sun.

Do not speak to me! Link
in the enduring flower
of an infinite love,
your hands and my hands,
your silence and mine.

Hush now! Breathe the blue,
listen to the gold.

142

Song

The setting sun flooded
my heart with bright coins of gold.
I arose, by night, to admire them:
But they were nothing worth!

With coins of silver, the moon
by daybreak filled my soul.
I closed my door, by day,
to look at them: nothing worth!

143

Song

I embellished my heart
with the roses of sleep,
and started on my way, blue-skyward.

All the stars were sitting in a row,
like little naked girls, ceaselessly
swinging their legs, in the blue,
on the rim of the sky.

When I arrived, they madly kicked
at my soul with their feet,
and laughing, pushed me back
to the confusing day of the awake.

144

Dream, dream, while you sleep;
with day you will forget.

—Day, merry apprenticeship
of infinite sophistry!

Learn, learn, while awake,
asleep you will forget.

—Sleep, sweet apprenticeship
of final forgetfulness!

145

(To Miss Rápida)

If you hurry,
time, like a darting butterfly,
will flee before you.

If you linger,
time, like a gentle ox,
will trudge behind you.

146

It was as lovely as in dreams.

Glory, descended,
by ladders of light
to the sunset of gold,
was playing in a garden by the sea.
And, transformed into love,
gave herself up to poetry.

     ... But it was truth!

147

Hours, golden ruins
of my yesterdays!
        I come, gentle,
to sit with you,
facing the sea, in the valley, under the sky
of my memories.

The grass, so like
the grass of other years, with sunlight through it,
makes me weep. And tears
flood my future
and drown me in the griefs that are no more.

It is a gentle drowning,
that draws me to itself, tenderly,
as things draw us that we
let go and do not join,
under the sky, in the valley, over the seas ...

148

I know I am the trunk
of the tree of the eternal.
I know that with my blood
I nourish the stars;
that every shining dream
is a bird of my owning . . .
I know that when the ax
of death strikes me down,
the firmament will fall.

149

O joy without reason!
will you be true to me?

Since all that thinks forgets,
whatever is felt passes,
joy without cause or meaning,
be constant!

150

Deluge

I wept, I wept, I wept until I drowned the world
in a new flood.
I saved only my heart,
that its race might not die.

My heart opened its blood
and the dove flew away . . .
                    Did I sleep?
                              O star
of dawn! . . . No, white dove
that from my heart took flight, in sleep;
don't return to heaven now; give
to my true life
your branch of light!

151

I am like an inattentive child,
dragged by the hand
through the world's carnival.
My eyes cling sadly
to things . . .
And how it hurts when I am dragged away from them!

152

Every autumn life
affirms, in slow martyrdom,
the ideal.

Arrogant blaze,
immortal spring,
of fire that gives gold,
of gold that gives light,
of light that gives death,
of death that gives to God eternal life!

153

Immortal word of mine!
Oh, what a supreme living
—when the tongue in my mouth is nothingness—
oh, what a divine living
of flower without stem and root,
nourished by light, with my memory,
alone and fresh within the breath of life!

PIEDRA Y CIELO (1917–1918)

154

The Poem

I uproot the bush,
still covered with the dew of dawn.

Oh, what a spray of earth,
odorous and moist,
what a shower—a dazzle—of stars
on my brow, in my eyes!

155

What an immense tearing to shreds
of all my life,
just to be, complete,
in each thing;
not to stop being,
with all of me, in each thing!

156

Remembrance I

(1)

This instant
that is to be a memory, what is it?
Wild music
bringing back these colors that are not
—since they were
part of that day of gold and love and glory;
what is this music
that is soon not to be?

(2)

Instant, endure, be a memory
—memory, you are more, for you go on
without ending, beyond death with your arrow—
be a memory, with me now far away!
. . . Oh yes, to go on, on, not be an instant,
but have perennial life in memory!

(and 3)

Immense memory of mine,
of instants that were centuries ago;
eternity of the soul of death!
. . . Instant, pass on, pass, you who are—alas—
I!
What is this instant, this you,
which you will be on dying?

157

Remembrance II

Memories are like golden dunes
of sand that come and go.

The wind takes them away,
and where they are, they are,
and they are where they were,
and where they are to be . . . Golden sand dunes.

They fill it all, total
sea of ineffable gold,
with all the wind within it . . . —Memories.

158

Remembrance III

(1)

Please do not leave, remembrance, do not leave!
Face, do not dissolve
thus like death!
Continue watching me, great eyes, fixed
as for one moment that you gazed at me!
Lips, smile at me,
as once you smiled at me a moment's span!

(2)

O brow of mine, press close;
do not permit her form
to be dispersed outside its continent!
Press close her smile, her glance,
till they become my very inner life!

(3)

—Though I forget myself,
though my face may take, from touching hers,
the shape of her face;
though I be her own self,
though my being may be lost in her—

(4)

O memory, be I!
You—she—be memory all and only, evermore!
memory to regard me, smile at me
in nothingness;
memory, life with my life,
become eternal by obliterating me!

159

Remembrance V

The river is flowing under
my soul, undermining me.
I can barely remain
upright. The sky
does not support me. Stars
deceive me; no, they are not
above, but down below, there in the depths . . .

Am I? I will be!
I will be, made wave
of the river of memory . . .

With you, flowing water!

160

How we are not alone!
How we deceive each other, in one another, always,
with the commingled blood
of sentiment! How one laughs and weeps
with the others!
            Subtle threads
that are left to bind us each to each
after our unbinding;
so that we nevermore may be alone;
smiles, kisses, tears!

161

Uphill

Immense flowering almond tree,
white-crowned in the silence filled with moonlight,
your trunk black in the total hush of shadow;
how, as I climb the bitter rock toward you,
you seem to sink your giant trunk
into the bowels of my flesh,
to star with my soul the firmament.

162

Daybreak

The sky, in the oblivion
of my sleep, had forgotten
to be what it is.

      I opened my eyes
suddenly, looked up, and a glory
open also, a garland of mysteries,
green, immaculate, blue,
wreathed my awakened brow.

The sky was not a name,
but sky.

163

Roses

Your love—how gaily—
singing, draws water with its fresh young arms
from the well of my heart.

The bucket knocks against my chest,
and cold, the hard water spills
—what gladness—on my soul.
The pulley chain is laughing
with a sparrow that hovers over you . . . —

Now your bucket is full
—how gaily—
at my mouth, the curbstone!
      . . . Your love—how gaily—
waters its roses with my heart.

164

Divine Hound

Here it is! Come all!
Dig, burrow!

My hands are running blood,
and I can dig no more!

Here it is!

Up from the moist earth,
scent of eternity!

Here it is!

Listen to my long baying
against the immortal sun!

Here it is! Come all!
Dig, burrow, dig!

165

Book

Book, desire
to be everywhere,
in solitude!

166

Seas

I feel this boat of mine
has struck, down in the depths,
against something large!
                    And nothing
happens! Nothing . . . Calmness . . . Waves . . .

—Nothing happens; or is it that everything
has happened, and we are, calm, starting anew?

167

Seaway

All are asleep, below.
                    Above, alert,
the helmsman and I.

He, watching the binnacle, keeper
of the bodies now in slumber. I,
my eyes on the infinite,
guiding the open treasures of the souls.

168

Dreamed Nocturne

Earth carries us through earth;
but you, sea,
carry us through the sky.

With what assurance of light of gold and silver,
the stars mark for us
the way—One might say
that the earth is the roadway
of the body,
that the sea is the highway
of the soul—

Yes, it seems
that the soul is the only voyager
of the sea; that the body, alone,
stayed behind there on the
shore, bidding it farewell,
heavy, cold, as if dead.

How similar
the voyage on the sea to the one toward death,
toward eternal life!

169

A butterfly of light,
beauty departs when I arrive
at its rose.

I run, blind, after it . . .
I almost catch it here and there . . .

In my hand I hold only
the image of its flight!

170

Brief song, brief song;
many, many;
like stars in the sky,
like sands on the shore,
like weeds in the meadow,
like waves in the river . . .

Brief song; brief ones, many;
hour, hours, hours, hours
—stars, sands, weeds,
waves—hours, lights; hours,
shadows; hours of the lives,
of the deaths of my life . . .

171

Treasures of the blue,
that one day and another, in frequent flight,
I bring to earth! Dust of the earth,
that, one day and another, I carry to the sky!

Oh, how rich are the hands of life
laden with flowers from on high!
How pure, each star,
from burning up sorrows of life!
—Oh, I, how rich, giving to all
everything I gather and change with my dreams!—

What happiness this daily flight,
this liberal service,
from the earth to the sky,
from the sky—O bird—to the earth!

172

Yes—says the day. No
—says the night—

Who strips the petals from this immense daisy
of gold, white, and black?

And when, say, Lord of the uncreated,
will you believe we love you?

173

Nocturne

My tear and the star
touched each other; at once
they became one single tear,
they became one single star.

I was blinded, and the sky
was blinded by love.
All—and nothing else—was
grief of star, light of tear.

174

The Moment

I am losing it, losing it, losing it!
... It is gone!
                    And with the moment
I lost eternity!

175

(1)

Today when I opened my eyes
to the light, I thought
—for the first time—
contentedly—my heart—of death.

(2)

It was like being born
again, a half-birth,
between the first
and the last birth, death.
                    And memories
of my former life have all been burned
in the great sun of forgetfulness.

(3)

A second life, this,
so serene, unadorned,
with my whole consciousness
on everything—and I standing
by my own side—forever,
above the pure fountain
of eternity.
                    Second
life, real life
of here below; complete dominion;
maturity of the mind
—youthfulness of the heart—harvest time
of the soul, fruit of the flesh!

(and 4)

. . . Now what a tranquil
beginning once again along the path
with firm foundation toward everything,
. . . or, it's all the same, toward nothingness!

176

Annunciation

Oh, to be dissolved,
once and for all in light;
to enter, become green ultimate gold,
in the free concealed secret
of impossible ardors!

177

I wish my book might be
as is the sky at night,
all present truth, without history.

That, as the sky, it might give itself
at every moment, with all its stars; nor
should childhood, youth, old age detract
or add in charm to its great beauty.

Tremor, flash of light, music
present and total!
Tremor, flash of light, music in the mind
—heaven of the heart—of the pure book!

POESÍA (EN VERSO) (1917–1923)

178

Around the crown
of the tall tree,
my dreams are circling in flight.

They are doves, adorned
with pure lights,
spilling music in their flight.

How they go in and out
the lonely tree!
How they entangle me in gold!

179

Wakefulness

Night retreats, black bull
—full flesh of mourning, mystery, and fright—
that has bellowed terribly, immensely,
to the sweating fear of all the fallen;
and the day comes, fresh child,
asking trust, love, and laughter
—child that so long ago,
in secret places where
beginnings meet their endings,
played for a brief moment,
in some mysterious meadow
of light and shadow,
with the fleeing bull.

180

Outside

Oh, the stiff air,
bell pealing in the cold,
eyes on the frost!

Indoors, before,
the house was the body
and the body was soul.

Oh, the white earth,
the silence, smoke
it draws from the hearth!

Now, walking along,
the soul is the body,
the house is the soul.

181

At times I feel
like the rose
that I shall be, like the wing
that I shall be;
and a perfume shrouds me, alien and mine,
mine and a rose's;
and a wanderlust grips me, alien and mine,
mine and a bird's.

182

I no longer wanted the star,
and turned away my eyes;
but the star came in them;
like—I thought—a flower of snow.

But the snow flower was all essence
—all tears—of ermine; and it dissolved,
and fell, drop by drop, within me.

It overbrimmed, and I began to weep;
and I wept ermine and perfume to the black world
and a glory of melted stars.

183

Immortality

You, word of my mouth, given life
by this meaning that I give you,
become my body with my soul.

184

Everything nothing? And what of this full pleasure
of entering under the earth, finished
just like a lovely book?
And this supreme delight
of turning loose from life
like the perfect fruit from its branch?
And this unique gladness
of having left in the invisible
the complete reality of desire,
like a river that flows toward the sea,
its perennial sculpture?

185

How, death, am I to fear
you? Are you not here with me, working?
Do I not touch you with my eyes; don't you tell me
you know nothing, that you are hollow,
unaware, peaceful? Don't you enjoy
with me everything: beauty, solitude,
love, to your very marrow?
Are you not, for my sake, enduring
life, standing by me, death?
Don't I take you back and forth,
your blindman's guide? Don't you utter
with passive lips
what I want you to say? Don't you bear,
slave, the kindness with which I bind you?
What will you see, what say, where go
without me? Will I not be,
death, your death, whom you, death,
must fear, indulge, cherish?

186

Poetry; dew
of each dawn, child
of each night; fresh, unsullied
truth of the ultimate stars,
above the tender truth
of the first flowers!

Dew, poetry;
matinal drops from the heavens to earth!

187

Gentleness

Does the withered leaf hold
the light that enchants it,
or the light
the enchanted leaf?

188

Truth

I have now won from the world
my world. The former immensity
of others, becomes today
my immensity.

189

Hand Against the Light

We are nothing but a feeble bag
of blood and bones,
and a pin, it is true, can kill us;
but in us flows the seed
that may produce
the one butterfly,
of light only and of shadow only and only ours,
without skin, network, or frame,
nor possibility of being caught
by human or divine;
the invulnerable being,
incorporeal, as long as the world,
that brims, free, the infinite
and goes on to the impossible.

190

Voice of mine, sing, sing,
for as long as there is anything
that you have not said
you have said nothing!

142

191

Moguer Dawns

The lone black bull appears, clear, beautiful,
against the cool green dawn, high on the blue crag.
It bellows from south to north, pushing back
the darkly crimson zenith, covered still
by the largest stars,
with its gigantic head.

—The immense solitude is filled with fear;
the unending silence is hushed.

           . . . !

The bull—a broken boulder—plunges down
against the leafy gorge.

           Nothing remains but him,
going? all black,
and coming! in white and rose, the light.

192

Pre-Autumn

Tin-plated sun,
blue whitewashed walls!
The sidewalk pure
with lovely lights!

—The cool cyclone
absorbed in cleaning
the shallow prism
of golden world!

How many memories
—how many colors!
How well, beauty,
your light deflects!

193
We Three

Sleep, death,
my invisible brothers,
brothers in the deepest sense,
brothers in nothingness!

194

What happens to a melody
when the playing stops; what
to a breeze that stops
blowing, and what
to a light that goes out?

Tell me, death, what are you but a silence,
calm, and shadow?

195
Native Land

Whence is a leaf
transparent in the sun?
—Whence is a mind
that thinks, a heart that yearns?
Whence comes a torrent
that sings?

196

White cloud,
broken wing—whose?
that could not arrive—where?

197

Woman, with music,
seems of crystal—pomp of love—
laughter, teardrop,
transformed into
human lily,
with edges of fine light of stars.

Woman, with music, is music;
fountainhead of shadow
—the immense well—
which is our passionate heart,
profuse and rhythmical.

198

One day a man will come
who, pouncing on you, will try to strip
away your unknown word of mourning,
my word, today so stark, so clear!
A man who will believe you
shadow made water of rare murmuring,
you, my voice, water
of simple light!

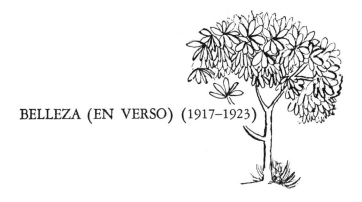

BELLEZA (EN VERSO) (1917–1923)

199

I know my work is the same
as a painting in the air;
that the hurricane of time
will erase it all, as though
it were perfume or music;
that there will remain of it
—one yes ruined by many noes—
in the great and sun-filled silence,
the ignorance of the moon.

—No, no; one day it will be
(erased) an immense existence,
a wakeful vigilant virtue,
it will be, like the presunrise,
impossible perfect norm;
an unending anguished zeal,
mine of sublime secrecy . . . —
My mortal immortal flower,
queen of the air today!

200

Moguer Dawns
Ríotinto

Santiago Watering Place

As the stagecoach enters town by the large bridge,
—a thoughtful silence, now fronting the station—
the river, full and red,
gathers still above San Juan the moon . . .

Infinite solitude
of coppery water between two bridges
—that dried up earth between two tunnels—
with never a boat!

. . . Afar, by Niebla—out of sight—the smoke
of the train, above the still mist-covered eucalyptus,
from Ruiza. The whitewashed wall,
ocher of copper, from Piquete inn,
little by little, sordid, becomes dazzling
under a hard sun, distorted, harsh . . .

The useless red water
of Ríotinto, between two bridges,
with never a boat!

201

To create, recreate, empty myself, until
what departs from me, dead, one day,
to earth, shall not be me; honestly to evade,
completely, with open will,
the crime, and leave to it this stuffed black dummy
of my body, in my place!
                    And I, hiding,
smiling, immortal, on the perfect shore
of the eternal river, tree
—in an unfading sunset—
of divine, magical imagination!

202

Ideal Epitaph

April! Alone, unsaddled,
white horse of my happiness?

—He came, trampling the dew-wet
rosebushes; dislodging all the rocks
of heavy waterfalls as he plunged in; waking,
cyclone of light, the happy birds—

Your panting, your lather, your sweat,
seem to come from another life . . .
Come to me, come to me, my horse;
April, April returning,
white horse
of my wandering love!

—My eyes caress him, holding close
his head white as the moon,
with its carbon black diamond—

April, April, what of your fair rider?
My poor love, my poor love, April!

203

I awoke beneath
the sky, poor fallen roof,
black and red of the night and of the dawn,
with spider webs, cinders, creeping beasts.

Arising, I arranged it as I could,
and, under its poor tent, still somewhat blue,
I slowly went to what was mine.

And that arrangement then I called my day.

204

Song

White Poplar

Above the bird is singing,
and the water sings below.
Above and below.
my soul is breaking—

The bird is rocking the star,
and the water rocks the flower.
—Above and below,
my soul trembles—

205
They

Foolish I! How
can this word of mine ever reach
the unspoken mystery of their souls?
How can my vain explosions light up
their inward skies
of a white gold that no reflected dawn
can reach?

Foolish I, yes; and happy they
in their muteness, in their perfect deafness!

206
The One Friend

It will be the same
—you alive, I in death—
as an appointment in the garden,
when the one who was waiting has to go
—how sadly—to his appointed lot
and he who was to come, comes
from where he was, late—and with what eagerness!

You will approach, and you will see only
the bench; and, yet, you will walk to it,
and look a little all around,
with saddened eyes, dazzled
by the inner sun of your scarlet west;
and then slowly, just as I did,
you will go, as far
from you, as I shall be.

207

The Little Green Bird

William Blake

How I live in the flame!
How I live!

Brief endless sun, I burn!
How I live!

Through my live coal shows the sky!
How I live!

Now appears my soul!
How I live!

208

Where is the word, heart,
to beautify with love the ugly world;
to give forever—and already only—
vigor of a child
and defense of the rose?

209

Music

In the tranquil night,
you are the rain, pure melody,
keeping the stars alive
—like lilies in a fathomless vase.

210

Early Morning

New cold: cock crowing.
Thunder and moonlight: child weeping.
Lonely street: dog slinking.
Night still: man thinking.

211

Latitude

If I were only a bit
of sea or sky; the same and different always, with the
    waves,
the same and different always, with the clouds;
firm and roving,
full of doubt and sure,
hopeful of companionship and wishing solitude,
known and a stranger,
loved and forgotten, free and captive
—different and the same always, with my clouds,
with my waves!

212

I wish to sleep, this night
that you lie dead; to sleep;
sleep, sleep, parallel
to your total sleep;
to see if I reach you, thus!

Sleep, dawn of the evening;
source of the river, sleep;
two days that may shine together
in nothingness, two currents
going, as one, to the end;
two wholes, if this life be something,
two nothings, if all is nothing . . .

I want to sleep your death.

213

Opus

Good-bye to you—to me, myself—left behind
—me left behind, how happily—on firm earth,
going away by sea; assured
against death by water!

Good-bye to you—to me—
                                    With what a smile

—as in a magical exchange of flowers—
we part, the mortal—I—the father,
from me, the immortal child!

214
Moguer Dawns
Pre-Summer

I never saw a higher sky,
nor happier wind than that rose-colored wind,
against that giant poplar—still greenish-brown
upon its river's edge—
that bowed submissively, awakening
—like nakedness of love before another nakedness—
that rippled all along the cooling edges,
filled with little birds that did not leave,
laughing interminably,
enjoying without pause, and singing
intoxicated with shadow and light,
singing . . .

215

Port

Asleep: our body
is the anchor
that our soul leaves
in the depth of the sea of our life.

216

Figurations

I thought already lost
my heart in me, this "knock, knock,"
dry and hard, that slips
a distinct me in me; and I lay down to sleep,
gently, beside my body.
                           But suddenly
—at fall of that contradictory day—
among the thickets of the gorge,
it rose—"knock, knock"—once more, beneath me,
in a confused explosion of hoofs and neighings,
indomitable steed, alien, wild!

217

Zenith

I shall not be myself, Death,
until you are one with life
and thus complete my whole;
until my light-half merges
with my shadow-half
in the balanced penumbra of eternity
         —in the mind of the world:
sometimes my light half, radiance,
and then my shadow-half, oblivion—

I shall not be myself, Death
until in your turn you deck
my soul with pallid bones.

218

Woman, oh, swift brush fire!
Much flame
suddenly . . .
          Then, nothing!

219

Corporeal Autumn

This death matters not to me—
it is but the body's fall.
I shall not die when I die—
not in the way things die here.

—What happiness not to know
just what death shall be my death,
nor in what century—or whether
in this or some future day.

A joyful thing, this victory—
this not knowing one's own death,
the real, real dying.

CANCIÓN (1935)

220

The Rain-Bird

Oh, singing rain-bird,
what chant you, enchant you?

To the approaching evening
you give a nostalgia
of fresh eternity
and of rain-drenched glory.
And the sun disrobes
at your canticle.

Oh singing rain-bird!

From the rosebushes
of my garden, you call
to those lovely clouds
overbrimming tears.
I should like to see
silver drops on the roses.

Oh singing rain-bird!

My song too has been
the song of the rain.
In my springtide
the gray cloud comes down
to water the roses
of my hopes.

Oh singing rain-bird!

I love the blue and wandering
sound that you scatter
on the greening leaves,
on the fountain's white.
Do not go away,
wingèd heart!

O singing rain-bird,
what chant you, enchant you?

221

To God in Spring

Dear Lord, kill me if Thou wilt.
(But Lord, please do not kill me!)

Lord, for rich sounds manifold,
for the butterfly of gold,
for the rose with morning star,
for cuckoos running in the path,
for the nightingale's sweet throat,
and for the flowering orange groves,
for the river's pearls of spume,
for the pine grove's lingering gloom,
for her red lips newly wise,
and for her new-seeing eyes . . .

Lord, dear Lord, do not kill me!
. . . (but do kill me if Thou wilt.)

222

They

Along the black depth
of the night they go.
Pure white roses
of noble perfume
glow brightly in the cold
of night's darkness.

(They go slowly, thinking . . .
And why should they think?)

Their life is all they wish.
They desire only
their hearts united,
joined in peace.
Their lips much closer,
their eyes as one.

(They go sweetly laughing . . .
and I wonder why?)

O celestial grace
of love! By virtue
of their submissiveness
let them live (on earth!)
an eternity.

223

The Absent One

Close, close the door,
the way she liked it.
Let her memory
feel at home!

224

Night

Sleeping is like a bridge
joining today to tomorrow.
Underneath it, like a dream,
flows the water, floats the soul.

225

I did not wish to subdue
your weakness, but your strength.

That torture, that slow
path of beauty,
was so clear and pure
for noble understanding!

(How divinely sang the bird
its heavenly song of faith!
And charity was not there.
And how the wayside flower
held out its gift of hope!)

Broad highway, so long
and so sweet, forever open!
Hidden, certain short-cut,
so short, and yet so bitter!

I did not wish to proffer you
my weakness, but my strength.

226

Rhythm

Cast off the rock of today,
forget and sleep. If it be
light, you will find at dawn
tomorrow that it is sun.

227

Memories*

Like golden dunes of sand
that now come, now go
in the wide sea of light,
             are memories.

The wind takes them away.
And where they are, they are,
and are where they once were
and where they are to be . . .
             (Golden sand dunes.)

They fill everything, a total
sea of unsounded gold,
with all the wind within . . .
             (Such are memories).

* A slightly different version of this poem appears in *Piedra
y Cielo.*

228
Four

Three gave him gall:
the one behind,
the one beside,
the one before him.

Life shouted
with the light between:
"How ugly is the fair!"

To three he gave honey:
to the one before him,
to the one beside
to the one behind.

And life sang
with the light between:
"How fair the ugly!"

229
Roundness

To caress a shoulder,
to caress the wave
to caress the cloud,
to caress the rock.

The human hand with light
upon the soul with form.
Melody of the touch,
rounded eternity.

230

Tranquil Valley

The dead sleeping
his profound truth,
puts forth the gray rose
gray rose of peace.

Blood in its chalice;
faith in the final light
that lights the air,
that soothes the sea.

And living man yearns
in his solitude
for calmest wave of
immortal life.

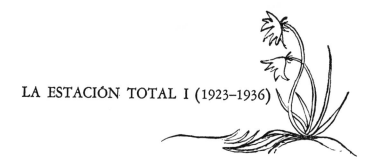

LA ESTACIÓN TOTAL I (1923–1936)

231
From Within

It shattered my soul with gold.
And like a magic palm tree
reclining in its light,
caressed me, gazing into my eyes
from deep within.

It told me with its eyes:
"I will be plenitude
of your middle hours.
I shall boil away your tedium,
and make foam of your doubts."

Since then, what peace!
I no longer hold out
my hands. The infinite
is within. I am
the horizon drawn in.

Woman, Poetry, Love, the indubitable
center.

Autumn Fruit

I am fulfilled with nature,
in full dusk of gold maturity,
high wind transfixed upon the green.
Rich hidden fruit, I hold
in me the elemental great (earth,
water, fire, and air) the infinite.

Light streams from me: I gild the darkened place;
I seep fragrance: the shadow smells of god;
I distill sound: space is profound music;
I filter savor: the mass drinks up my soul;
I delight the touch of solitude.

I am treasure supreme, unfettered,
with the dense roundness of a limpid opal,
from the bosom of action. And I am all:
The all that is the peak of nothingness,
the all that is enough and that is served
with what is still but ambition.

233
Condition

The pine consoles itself
with rain; the rose
with the greenfinch; man
with woman, the star,
the orange?

Nothing knows to what rival
ether it goes or aspires,
nothing, no one desires
but love (more than oblivion).

. . . Instant of emptiness,
and the ugly appears.

But vibrate, light,
but enter, shadow,
and dazzle and quench
the interfering spy!

234

Plenitude

In front is emotion's crimson hue.
And in the depths of life,
through the soft cloudy blue,
among the last copper-colored leaves
that curve in ecstasies of glory,
eternal plenitude unveiled.

(And the one water is more visible.
Color is more itself, only itself,
odor alone has greater breadth,
color is more audible.
                   And in the air,
in the water, above the heat,
above the odor, above color, before
the crimson of the second passion, cries
external plenitude unveiled.)

Unending harmony, great harmony
taking its leave without a care,
in light of gold that will soon turn to green,
that is yet to see so many times,
before the crimson glow of reverie,
internal plenitude unveiled!

235

Relative Blue

It sprang from the night. I say to it
"I will catch you, I will know you."

                           And I leap

after it.
        Our shadows
enlarged, filled out, exalted,
entwine or flee each other,
passing their unreal form among the roses,
are taken as a faction by a star,
losing themselves when about to meet, in the water.

"Yes, it was you," it says.
                       And instantly
the you is forgotten in the dark,
the you that was, that was to be, had been,
the you of it, mine, ours;
the yes that, in the depth
of the great garden of forgetfulness,
lives in the magic palace,
with fatal secret, of the memory.

"It is you, it was you," I say,
"and I, was I, am I, myself to you?"

A chill between the two eliminates us,
the chill of utter no.

And I leap from the night
into my shelter which was my truth,
the truth of the submissive and resigned.

And everything in my sight appears small,
thick wall of rigid blue,
the relative blue, the poor blue,
flat, the same as yesterday, same as before!

Returning Flower

Faithful, the flower returns
to limit our blue moment,
to give a willing kinship to our body,
to say to us, in all its immense fragrance,
that the brief moment is enough.

The brief moment in sun of gold, in golden air,
in golden earth, in golden sea;
beside the heaven of the gods,
within the obscure no,
in sufficient energy,
in harmony and in light.

And the flower sways, with the richest
fragrance of the flesh,
fragrance that invades the being to reach the end
of its endlessness, and there is lost,
making for us a garden.
The living flower sways, inside and out,
with weight exactly suited to its pleasure.
The bird loves it and gives it ecstasy,
and woman roundly loves it,
and man loves it and kisses it between.

To blossom and to live, instant
of central spark withheld,
wide open in a tempting, luring form;
instant without a past,
in which the four cardinal points
are of equal attraction, sweet and deep;
instant of love wide open
as the flower!
Blossom and love in perfection of form,
in mutual frantic yes of oblivion,

in a mad compensation;
odor, savor and odor,
color, odor and touch, odor, love and fragrance.

The crimson wind persuades it,
enticing it away, delicious rape,
with a sharp fall, which is a dying
of sweetness, of tenderness, of coolness;
fall of the flower in its total beauty,
a flying, passing, dying of love and flower
in beauty's greatest day,
without grieving the world in ardent going,
with sun and shadow mellowing the earth,
becoming lost within the eyes of light!

237
Poet and Word

When the air, supreme companion,
occupies the place of those now gone,
dissipates their fragrance, gestures, sounds,
and is again the only one to fill
the natural sequence of their silence,
he, to whose infinite limits
midnight and midday bind themselves
(horizons of absent silver and gold beyonds)
remains with the air in his place,
gently pressed by the atmosphere
of the blue eternal attribute.

He may forget, be silent, cry within
the word that reaches from the rounded whole,
the only rounded whole;
that the encircled center will hear
always resolved and forevermore;

that remains light and firm above all things;
the vibrant, silent word,
the immanent one,
sole flower that does not bend,
sole light that does not dim,
sole wave without a break.

From all the white, black secrets
comes to him in echo, full of love,
full and lofty with all its treasures,
the profound, silent, true
word,
that only he has heard, hears, will hear in his vigilance.
His flesh and soul, unique, in his atmosphere
then are word:
beginning and end,
present with no more a backward glance,
destiny, flame, fragrance, stone, wing, defenders,
life and death,
nothingness or eternity: then word.

And he is the god rapt in the principle,
complete without having said a word;
the intoxicated god of what is to be,
inexhaustible in his precise naming;
the unanimous god in the end,
happy repeating everything each day.

CANCIONES DE LA NUEVA LUZ (1923–1936)

238–242

The Hidden Victor

(1)

I Live

I live. And my blood
is burning up loveliness.

Live. And my double blood
is evaporating love.

I live. And my blood
is refining consciousness.

(2)
On the Rock

What solitude, what desert?
Are you not water, am I not wind?

What darkness, what boredom?
Am I not lightning, are you not lily?

What emptiness, what island?
Are you not soul, am I not life?

(3)
Life, Thanks, Death

Thanks, life, for I have been able
to enter the secret of the spirit.

(Thanks because I have tried
to reach the infinite.)

Thanks, Death, for I have been able
to stand within the sea of idealism.

(4)
Second Creator

What do I care, dry sun?
I make the blue fount in myself.

Dim snow, so what?
I make within my heart the crimson forge.

What do I care, smoke love?
I make the eternity of love in my soul.

(5)
Light and Black

What a mine this of my light,
treasure of this darkness!

Shadow far above the sky,
shadow through the midst of earth,
shadow far beneath the sea.

Gold in my enfolding mind,
gold within my total heart!

243
Flowers Under Lightning

The flowers hold hands
and fly like the birds.
They don't leave.
(But they fly like the birds.)

They pull, lift their heads down there,
under the great storm cloud.
They don't leave.
(Under the great storm cloud.)

They cry with pain and with white,
with yellow and with tears.
They don't leave.
(With yellow and with tears.)

Each thunder clap with its dart
draws cries at the lightning flash.
They don't leave.
(They cry at the lightning flash.)

Bitten, their odor is so great
that the soggy fragrance bleeds.
They don't leave.
(Their soggy fragrance bleeds.)

They fly, for the birds escape,
so as not to die with fright.
They don't leave.
(So as not to die with fright.)

The flowers hold hands
and cry just like the birds.
They don't leave.
(But they cry just like the birds.)

244–245

Doomed Creator

(3)
My Realm

Only in eternity could
I realize this yearning
for complete beauty.

Eternity where there would
be neither note nor light
nor taste to say
"enough!" to my wing of life.

(Where the double stream
of my living and dreaming
would exchange the blue and gold.)

(and 4)
God First

Null days, like the days
of slow indifference
of the precreating god.

(All things hard, all things whole,
mass of black disarray,
like an I that is just I.)

Suddenly, one day of grace,
all things see me with my eyes,
I break into worlds of love.

246–248

Luxury

(1)
Happiness

Look at the poppy
through the green-and-blue!

And the benign cloud
rounded full of light.

Look at the gay poplar
in the green-and-blue!

And the happy blackbird
with all of the light.

Look at the new soul
through the green-and-blue!

(2)
Your Nakedness

The rose:
your nakedness made grace.

The fountain:
your nakedness made water.

The star:
your nakedness made soul.

(3)
Sense and Element

Taste
of the winds with the sun!

Coolness
of the rocks with the sun!

Odor
of the waves with the sun!

Color
of the flames with the sun!

Murmur
of the blood with the sun!

249

The Star That Came

In the orange tree is the star.
See who can lay hands on it!

Hurry, come with the pearls,
and bring out the nets of silk!

Upon the roof sits the star.
See who can lay hands on it!

Oh, what fragrance of spring
its pome of eternal light!

The star is in someone's eyes.
See who can lay hands on it!

Through the air, in the grass,
take care, it may get lost!

Harbored in love is the star!
See who can lay hands on it!

250

This Other One

This other I that spies
all that I do
is he the noble human
or the evil one?

Does he lift me or subdue me;
is he my conscience
or my white serpent
(black temptress)?

Must I respect him
like myself,
or overthrow him,
as an enemy?

251

My Anguish

What floats over the earth is smoke,
not rain.
And its blue evaporates as
my anguish.

What soars through the air is mist,
not wing.
And its plumage dissolves as
my anguish.

What rises through the shadow is dream,
not soul.
And its gray disintegrates as
my anguish.

252–253

Orders

(1)
Rhythm

Go where the dawn
bids you, and the dusk
will welcome you.
The sunset, in gladness,
gives to perfect radiance
its immortal gold.

Roads well-ordered
by the happy peace
of faithful walking!
Hope sings,
charity flies,
faith laughs.)

Our rhythm has
the one key
to the great garden.
It opens paradise
and locks nothing else
but its following.

(and 2)
Dawn, May, Life

Dusk
is not black,
dusk become night.
If blood is what follows,
it is burgeoning scarlet.

Autumn
is not sere,
even full autumn.
If it is blood dripping,
it is sowing of gold.

Death
is not a pauper,
death fulfilled.
If it is blood in depth,
it is a king's mine.

254–255

The Excursion

(1)

My House

Among the open clouds,
the translucent sunset,
the colors, the murmurings
of eternal dwellings
that will open anon.

And behind the presence
of the magic background,
rises the silver sky, happiness
of all the taper stars
that will soon be lighted.

(and 2)
The Anxious One

I want to reach my end
in galleys of the earth,
loaded with scarlet roses
and with swallows all in black,
through a sea of air spangled
with clouds of spring,
when along the sunset shores
the stars of evening disrobe.

256

Wave Rhythm

Diamond cloud
against radiant blue;
precious greenness
against glorious sun . . .
Wind of ardor,
wave of love!

Heart replete
beside serene god;
dream lost
in light of neglect . . .
Blood of fragrance.
rhythm of love!

World stopped
against deepest blue;
imposing body
against present sun . . .
Fruit yet in flower,
wing of love!

257

Blue Flight

The sky courses through the green.
Blue flight, and rain of blue!
Sink your life in this sky
high and terrestrial, plenitude!

Heaven on earth, this was all.
Being in glory, without ascending!
Here the blue, and enter the green!
Not to miss, not to leave the earth!

Soul and body between sky and sea.
Everything live with brightest light!
This is the end and was the source!
The water blue, and blue the flight!

258–260

In One Center

(1)
Peak

Cloudless now
my understanding
(O clear breeze!)
how well I see you!

Serene region
with all the least,
with all the most
of the supreme!

Below, black
(narrow valleys)
rounds echo
cries and thunder.

(2)
Movement

Trunk like the air,
breast like the sky.
Gulf,
oar.

Peace, harmony,
grandeur and height.
Bosom,
music.

This infinity
that darkness yearns for!
Crown,
fruit.

(and 3)
Being One

Let nothing invade me from without,
let me hear only myself within.
I, god
of my breast.

(I, all: sunset and dawn;
love, friendship, life, and dream.
I alone
universe.)

Pass on, do not think of my life,
leave me withdrawn and lean.
I, one
in my center

261

You Light

Vertical light,
light you;
you high light,
gold light;
vibrant light,
light you.

And I the black, blind, deaf, mute, horizontal shadow.

LA ESTACIÓN TOTAL II (1923–1936)

262
Rose of Shadow

Whoever it was did not see me, his shadow did,
coming exact and warm to cast a glance
into my half-closed life,
gray essence no longer fragrant;
wave in which two eyes formed one enlarged immensely.

(Shadows that see completely and receive
no glance. They alarm us, but are invulner-
ably smooth as oil.

With their spirals of exact foreshortening they invent
every possible act of espionage,
of introduction, of involvement.

They surprise without fear,
bite without lips,
leave without commitment.

At times they have left us a rose,
gray essence no longer fragrant,
sensual vise of nameless faith.)

A rose of shadows and of shadow,
my hand slimly extended,
music without sound, self-conscious smile,
by body that saw not,
I keep in my open hand.

Intimate Rose

(All roses are the same rose,
love! The only rose. And
everything is contained in it,
brief image of the world,
love! the only rose.)

Rose, the rose . . . (But that one rose . . .)
Spring returns
with the scarlet
rose, pink, yellow, white, scarlet;
and everyone is drunk with the rose,
the rose just like the other rose.
Is any rose like any other rose?
Are all the roses just the self-same rose?
Yes (but that rose . . .)

The rose that is held apart in a hand,
whose scent is breathed to its depth and to one's own,
the rose designed for the breast of love,
for the lips of love and for its soul.
(. . . And for the soul was that particular rose
that sweetly hid among the roses,
and that one evening was no longer seen.
What yellow color was the fresh-blown rose?)

All things, from rose to rose, frenetic live,
the light, the wing, the air,
the wave and woman,
and man, and man and woman.
The rose is there, fair
and delicate, for all,
its body without shadow, without secret,

at once full and smooth,
intimate, evident, ardent and gentle.
This rose, that rose, the other rose . . .
Yes (but that one rose . . .)

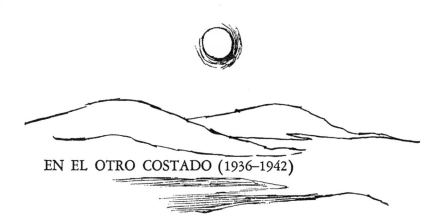

EN EL OTRO COSTADO (1936–1942)

264

The Birds from I Know Where

All night long
the birds have been singing
their colors to me.

(Not the colors
of their morning wings
with the freshness of the suns.

Not the colors
of their vesper breasts
in the embers of the suns.

Not the colors
of their everyday beaks
that lose their light at night,

as fade
the known colors
of the leaves and of the flowers.)

Other colors,
of the primal paradise
that man so completely lost,
paradise
that the flowers and the birds
know so well.

Flowers and birds
that come and go wafting scents,
flying through the whole wide world.

Other colors,
of that changeless paradise
that man in dreams wanders through.

All night long
the birds have been singing
their colors to me.

Other colors
which they have in their other world
and which they bring out at night.

Colors
that I have seen wide awake
and which are I know well where.

I know whence
the birds have come to
sing to me through the night.

I know whence
passing through winds and waves,
to sing my colors to me.

265

Strange Abyss

Blue air with blue sunlight,
well of an infinite light
with curbstone of new rock,
on fire my being flies
to your depth, wishing to reach
your highest depth.

Well I know I was created
for the deep and the high,
and that I live in a time
when only love can
kindle the eagerness
for the highest depth.

And I know that love gives
more light to this restlessness
that consumes me; and I love it,
for rising in its fire
my flames are able to reach
the highest depth.

Questions to the Resident

First question:
    You walking by on the stones,
have you an inner root too?

    Are you and your soil mingled,
as I, with another soil?

    Have you too an outward root,
you passing by with the wind?

    Does the dream you ponder on
return to you as its core?

Second one:
    This dark cloud that crushes me,
is it also crushing you?

    Did the embers the sun quenched
fall in your garden too?

    The emptiness of this height,
is it to you as to me?

Third one:
                (to the pine men)
    Are you here as you are there,
do you tell man the same thing?

    Does the infinite magnetize
your treetops just the same?

    Your murmur in the wind,
is it quiet, is it quiet?

    Is there only one pine grove,
and one this and that one, pines?

Fourth one:
  Against the dull, leaden sky,
do you remain in the house?

  You wait comfortably here
for the death of your tomorrow?

  Does one also go from here
to eternity without a country?

and Fifth one:
  Those crimson cirrus clouds, what
paradise do they restore?

  You who can see them from here,
how do they concern you?

  What oceans carry your foot,
your eyes what mountains shatter?

  Confusion of airs and faith,
decomposition of suns!

267

Ultimate Child

Faithful music in the scale
of strata, along the fleeting
sunset, against the space
of slow, smooth infinite.

With it my foot moves along
agile and firm, as
along the unending sand
of my brimming childhood dream.

Is there a white town there
waiting for me, full of light,
town where everything stops,
one square with one cry;
with a crystal cry,
a long, sharp cry,
ultimate cry in the end
of cloud, a yellow cry?

The cry has in its center
everything the child has seen,
everything he wished to see,
everything he has not seen.

The child is all the people,
the child is I as a child,
it is I as an old man,
it is a child found and lost.

ROMANCES DE CORAL GABLES (1939–1942)

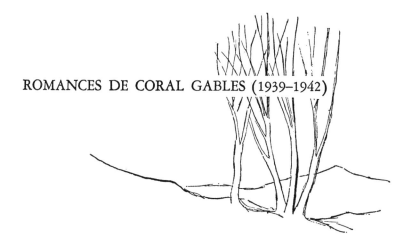

268

With Your Stone

The sky weighs as much
as a quarry of stone.
Above the stone of the world
the stars are made of stone.

This enormous weight
of rigid stone aflame!
Stone all of the stars,
stones, stone, stones, stone.

I travel between two stones,
I lie between stone and stone;
stone under my breast
and stone upon my head.

If I try to lift them up,
the eternal stone wounds me;
If I step in despair,
I bleed on the earthly stone.

What pain in my soul, stone;
flesh, what a stony pain;
what a jail is night, a walled
stone and wall of stone.

You threaten me with your stone,
destiny of stone and stone.
With your stone I shall hit
you on your crown of stone.

269

Entity

It is climbing toward otherness.

Up above, where the wind,
upon a line of the world,
total flight, glows with heat,
it sleeps, in the rock, dreamless.

And the loneliest birds
sing as for no one,
come down as for all,
to the no one in the all,
to the one in nothingness.
Absolute felicity:
the being of supreme nonbeing,
the nonbeing of supreme being.

Entity constant to oblivion,
forgetfulness in the glory

of the god that is nowhere
from long being without knowing,
and overbrims solitude.

That successive nonbeing
that is this one real being;
that nobody can transform,
that nobody can remove,
that nobody can avoid.

And a single flower sways
above the immense presence
of the authoritative absence.

270

Men Trees

Yesterday evening
I returned with the clouds
drifting under the rosebushes
(great, round tenderness)
among the faithful tree trunks.

The solitude was eternal
and the silence never-ending.
I stood still like a tree
and listened to the trees talking.

Only the bird took flight
from such a secret place,
I alone could stand there
among the last of the roses.

I did not wish to become
myself again, fearing
to displease, being different,
the trees that were alike.

The trees finally forgot
my shape of wandering man,
and I, my shape forgotten,
heard the talking of the trees.

I delayed until star-rise.
In a flight of softened light,
I began edging away,
with the moon now in the air.

When I was almost outside,
I saw the trees look at me.
They realized everything
and it grieved me to leave them.

And I could hear them talking,
among mother-of-pearl clouds,
in a soft murmur, about me.
How could I undeceive them?

Tell them that it was not so,
that I was only a passer-by,
that they must not talk to me?
I did not want to betray them.

And quite late, yesterday evening,
I heard the trees talk to me.

ANIMAL DE FONDO (1949)

271

Transparence, God, Transparence

God of what is to come, I feel you in my hands,
here you are involved with me, in love's sweet
strife, just like
fire with air.

You are not my redeemer, nor exemplar,
not my father, my son, nor my brother;
you are one and the same, distinct and whole;
you are god of the beautiful attained,
my consciousness of beauty.

I have nothing to purge.
All my encumbrances
are only the foundation of today
when, at last, I desire you;
for you are now beside me,
in my electric zone,
as full love is in love.

You, essence, are consciousness;
mine, others, everyone's,
with supreme form of conscience;
for essence is perfection,
the supreme form
and your essence is in me, as my form.

All my molds were filled
with you; but you, today,
are without mold, you are moldless; you are grace
that admits no support,
that admits no crown,
that crowns and supports in weightlessness.

You are unfettered grace,
the glory of pleasure, the eternal sympathy,
the joy of earthquake, the luminary
of clairvoyance, the depth of love,
the horizon that takes nothing away;
transparence, god, transparence,
the one at last, god now wonted in my oneness,
in the world that because of you and for you I have
        created.

272

Of Our Natural Movements

You are not only among men,
longed-for god; but you are here in the sea
(deserted more than ever of men)
waiting for man's natural coming, my coming,
because the sea, so neglected, is
our world of water.

Here you shape yourself in permanent
movement of lights and colors,
visible image of this movement
of your own becoming and of ours.

Here you shape
yourself, become abstract anxiety, substance
of all that consciousness that you are.

You are here in the sea, as now completely formed,
as if awaiting, in perfect faith
in our natural movements.

You are here as model and as mirror
of the imagination, my imagination in motion,
you are in triple incorporeal element,
water, air, high fire,
with the earth secure in all the horizon.

273

In My Third Sea

In my third sea you were
of that color made of all the colors
(as I said once before of your white);

in that murmur made of all the murmurs
that I always pursued, as I did color,
through air, earth, water, fire, love,
behind the terminal gray of all departures.

You were, you came to be, you are love
in fire, water, earth, and air,
love in my man's body and in woman's body,
the love that is the total
and only shape

of the natural element, which is the element
of everything, the forevermore;
and which has always held you and will hold you,
only all do not see you,
only we who look at you do not see you until one day.

Love most complete, love itself, are you,
with all the substance
(and with all the essence)
in all the senses of my body
(and in all the senses of my soul)
which are the same in the great knowledge
of one who, as I now, knows all in light.

Knows it, since he knew it more and more;
the most, the most, the only road to wisdom;
now I know that I am complete,
for you, my longed-for god, are visible,
are audible, are palpable
in murmur and in color of the sea, now:
because you are the mirror of myself
in the world, greater because of you, which is my world.

274

All the Clouds Are Burning

All the clouds are burning
because I have found you,
 longing and longed-for god;
tall purple torches
(scarlet, blue, red, yellow)
in shrill clamor of the voice of light.

From the round horizon they all come
in shining congregation,
to cling with a return of hope
to my justified faith.

(Desert sea, with god
in full consciousness
that speaks and sings to me,
that makes me confident, assured;
through you I walk along
alert, self-possessed,
content that my wayfaring
is toward the man pursued, who waits for me
at the port of permanent arrival,
of repeated encounters.)

All the clouds that were,
that are and that will be,
surround me with signs of evidence;
they are for me
the affirmation lifted from this deep
depth of air in which I live;
the true ascent of the ascent,
the ascent of the discovery in the deep height.

275

The Fruit of My Flower

This consciousness that surrounded me
in all my living life,
like a halo, aura, atmosphere of my very self,
has now come inside me.

Now the halo is within
and my body is visible
center of myself; visible, I am
the mature body of this halo,
as the fruit, which was the flower
of itself, is now fruit of my flower.

The fruit of my flower am I, today, because of you,
yearned-for and yearning god,
always green, blooming, in fruit,
golden, snowy, turned green
again (total season all at once)
with no more time nor space
than has my breast, this
head that I feel throbbing,
all of it my body and soul
(always with the seed
of the most ancient heart).

God, now am I the sheath of my core,
of you within me.

276

Full Consciousness

You bear me, full consciousness, yearning god,
throughout the world.
                    In this third sea,
I almost hear your voice; voice of the wind,
total occupant of movement;
of colors and of lights
eternal and marine.

Your voice of white fire
in the totality of water, boat, and sky,
limning the roadways with delight,
engraving with splendor my sure orbit
of black body
with the luminous diamond in its core.

To the Rayed Center

You are among the gold
cumulus of the blue sky,
the radiant cumulus
of the rounded horizon deserted
by foolish man,
yearning and yearned-for god;
these shapes that reach to the zenith
above the helm, move forward, and mark the rhythm
of the slow exalted movement,
the stately nodding of a prow,
crossing with its ascent, descent,
against the south, against the south,
erect, erect like a panting breast.

You come with my north toward my south,
you come from my east toward my west,
you come with me, lone crossroads, and you guide me
between the four immortal points,
leaving me in their center always and in my center
which is your center.

Everything is directed
to this palpitating treasure,
yearned-for and yearning god,
of my mine in which my diamond waits;
to this rayed motion
of inward being open (in its soul) with the sun
of day, which permeates you in ecstasy,
to the night, in the most heady interchange
known, of love and infinity.

278

Consciousness Blue Today

(God is bright blue . . .
Earlier)

Consciousness of the deep blue of the day, today
concentration of blue transparency;
sea that climbs to my hand to give me thirst
of sea and sky on sea,
in all-embracing waves, of vivid salt.

Morning of truth in a background of air
(sky of water background
of another life still in immanence)
explosion adequate (cloud, wave, spray
of wave and cloud)
to take me, body and soul,
to the limit of all confines,
to be what I long for
and to be the you you long for in my longing,
consciousness today of vast blue,
yearning and yearned-for consciousness,
god today blue, blue, blue, and bluer,
just like the god of my blue Moguer,
one day.

279
Without Tedium nor Rest

If I have gone so much about the world,
it has been only and always
to find you, yearned-for god,
among so many heads, so many breasts,
of so many men.

(Gigantic city, great concourse,
coming back to me in gray mirage of water,
in this blue sun of the south of light,
of this yearning and yearned-for god,
eyes and eyes and eyes
with instantaneous flashes
of the eternal to come.)

So many motors of thinking and of feeling
(black, white, yellow, red, green
of body) with their soul
striving toward you,
becoming toward themselves,
being toward me,
unknowingly or knowingly I and they!

Universal design, in flames
of shadows and of lights inquiring
and expectant.
of shifting and adventurous fate's
immense watching eye that spies on you
with pain or gladness.

And I possessor, in the middle, now,
of your consciousness, god, for having waited for you
from my destined infancy,
with neither rest nor tedium.

280
The Form Left to Me

Between the poised masts and spars and the high cloud
that my porthole limits in full circle,
you appear, yearning god, smiling
with the early sunrise, to watch me waken;
and I waken smiling, I too
at this dreaming awake that beckons me.

Throughout all my dreams, god, in momentary
flashes, well-being of the sleeping,
you interpolated, desired one,
as the gold waves of this sea,
this certainty that now absorbs me—
my day with night, my night with day.

And now, changing the dream to action
what energy uplifts me
and obliges me to believe that what I do
is what I can, must, want to do;
this task I am so glad to tell you of,
to tell myself in every sort of way, in the form
left to me of all, for you!

With the Southern Cross

The Southern Cross lies down upon a cloud
and looks with diamond eyes
into my eyes that are deeper than love,
with a love as of one forever known.

It was, it was, it was
in all the blue sky of my subjective state;
its four eyes were the clean
conscience, the successive solution of a beauty
awaiting me already in the kite
that as a child I used to fly.

And I have come, now I have come,
in my penultimate journey of illusion
of the god conscious of me and mine,
to kiss its eyes, its stars,
with four separate kisses of pure love;
the first one, on the eyes that grace its head;
the second and the third, on the eyes of its hands,
and the fourth, on that eye of its lofty mermaid's foot.

The Southern Cross is holding wake for me
in my last innocence,
in my return to the child-god I was one day
in my Moguer of Spain.

And below, far below me on most exalted earth,
which reaches to my exactest probing,
a silent mother nourishes me,
as she nourished me upon her living lap
when I flew my white kites;
and she feels now with me all the stars
of the round, full, night eternity.

282

In Equality Sure of Expression

Is the dog barking at my conscience,
at my god in all conscience,
as at a moon of fair imminence?

Does he see it aglow, this immense night,
through the shadow spangled by all the stars,
protector of its southern cross,
which serve me as a mantle
drawn over me in eagerness and love?

(This mantle which I feel makes my light
eternal, my mysterious light, my light,
a sister happy with her light.)

The dog comes, and I stroke him;
he licks me, and gazes at me like a man,
with complete brotherhood
of the calm, signal night.

He feels (I am aware) that I bestow
the caress a dog has always expected,
the tranquil silent stroking
in equality certain of expression.

283
That Open Orbit

The birds of the air
rock in the branches of the clouds,
the birds of the water
rock in the clouds of the sea
(and wind, rain, foam, sun in turn)
as I, god, rock in the dashing
of wave and bough, wind and sun, foam and rain
of your happy rocking consciousness.

(Is not the greatest
joy of the divine in the human
to let itself rock in god, in the lingering
consciousness of god, in the mothered immanence
with its sure interminable swaying?)

To and fro, the movement
of the eternal returning, in its own self
and in one's own self;
that open orbit
that never changes course, open,
that never escapes itself, open
(because)
the closed does not exist in its infinity
though it be sheltering arms and source and glory.

284

In Loving Fulfillment

We are all calmly working:
the fireman, stoking; the watchman,
keeping watch; the helmsman, guiding;
the painter, painting; the wireless operator,
listening; the carpenter, hammering;
the captain, directing; woman,
attending, sighing, quivering.

. . . And I, yearned-for god, yearning;
I who am filling you, in loving
fulfillment in my last consciousness,
like the sun or the moon, god,
with a world all one for everyone.

285
In the Best I Have

Green sea and gray sky and the blue sky
and loving albatrosses on the wave,
and in everything, sun, and you in sun, watching,
yearning and yearned-for god,
lighting my coming with distinctive golds;
the coming of the one that I am now,
the one that even yesterday I doubted
could ever be in you as I am now.

What change of man in me, yearning god,
no longer doubtful of the legend
of so many talkers' god,
now a firm believer
in the story I myself created
from the beginning of my life for you.

Now I have come to this end
of a year in my natural life,
in my depth of air in which I hold you,
above this sea, depth of water;
this lovely blinding end
into which you are coming,
content with being yours and being mine
in the best that I have, my utterance.

286

The Internal All

I have arrived at a land of arrival.
Your own awaited me, desired god;
mine awaited me,
those who, in my yearning of so many years,
awaited me with you,
with me awaited you.

And what a light among them:
in noonday sun unforeseen and almost weeping,
over a dawn with its towers against red,
upon a night of enchanted desiring,
an evening of prolonged twilight,
a midday of sheltering leaden gray,
through early morning with overcast and a star!

What a light among eyes, lips, and hands;
what a springtime in heartbeat;
what a you among them, and you in us;
what a light, what perspectives
of breast and brow (youth, elder, child);
what singing, what talking,
embracing, kissing;
what a rapture of you in us
until we reach you,
to this you that you place over yourself
so that all may arrive along the ladder
of flesh and soul
to the unsleeping consciousness that is the star
that gathers and completes, unifying,
all the stars in the eternal whole!

The eternal all that is the internal all.

287

River-Sea-Desert

I have arrived beside you, river-sea,
desert-river-sea of wave and dune,
of simoon and tornado, also, god;
sea for the foot and for the arm,
with the wing on the arm and on the foot.

No one ever told me.
I come to you through me in my hour, and discover you;
I discover you with god, desiring god,
who tells me that you were always his,
that you were also always mine
and you offer yourself to me in his eyes
like a great vision that I needed.

You give me motion in solidity,
a slower motion, since I go
toward my arrested motion;
motion of placid consciousness
of love with more sand,
sand to carry underneath death
(the unending current I have said before)
as something incorruptible.

Through you,
desert-sea of the river of my life,
I make land of my sea,
I rejoice in this sea (I used to say
was not part of my land);
through you my animal background of air
becomes more even; and the image
of my becoming faithful to beauty
is becoming more even toward my end,
fusing energy with ecstasy.

Sea, that I may with my two hands
touch, take, fuse the rhythm of my written being,
equate it in the wave of sea and earth.

Through me, my river-sea-desert,
the image of my work in final god
is no longer the arrested wave,
but only the arrested earth
which was restless, restless, restless.

288

In the Circumsummit

You are, desired god, in the circumsummit,
overlooking everything,
the round and the high,
from the top of a black cloud open in sparks.

Everyone sees you; all of us see you:
from the flat roofs with open
sides; from balconies
and their cage of low impulse, restless foot;
from the rooms of sensitive
intelligence; from the hallways;
from the branches of the raw moment;
from the cellars of the faithful exiled.

You come to all through your thousand sides;
you live in all with your thousand echoes;
you have no spark that does not touch
a sad or happy eye.

You are standing crown that everyone
may take off from his feverish head
and leave it fallen back upon a kiss.

Because you love, yearning god, as I love.

289
With My Half There

My silver here in the south, in this south,
awareness in luminous silver, throbbing
in the clean morning,
when spring makes my inmost being flower!

My silver here, a reply of the silver
that dreamed this silver once in the clean morning
of my silver Moguer,
of my silver Port,
of my silver Cadiz,
when I sad child dreamed always
of beyond-the-sea, beyond-the-earth, beyond-the-sky.

And the beyond-the-sky was here
with this earth, the beyond-earth,
this beyond-sea, with this sea;
and here, in this beyond-sea, my manhood found,
north and south, his full consciousness,
for this he had lacked.

And I am happy with full happiness,
with my half there, my there, complementing me,
since I now have my totality,
my silver here in the south, in this south.

290
Just as You Were

In my memory you are just as you were.
My consciousness was already this consciousness,
but I was sad, always sad,
because my person was not yet similar
to this last consciousness.

Among those geraniums, under that lemon tree,
beside that well, with that young girl,
your light was there, yearning god;
you were beside me,
yearned-for god,
but you had not yet become a part of me.

The sun, the blue, the gold were,
like the moon and the stars,
your sparkling and your whole coloration,
but I could not seize you with your essence,
the essence fled from me
(like the butterfly of form)
for the form was in me
and running after the other I would leave it;
so long, so faithfully I carried it.
that it seemed not to me what it was.

Today, thus, without my knowing why,
I have it whole, whole.
I know not on what day nor with what light
it came to a garden, perhaps, to a house, sea, mountain,
and I saw it was my name without my name,
without my shadow, my name,
the name that I had before I was
hidden inside this being that wearied me,
for it was not this being that I have today fixed
(that I might not have fixed)
for all the illuminated, illuminating
future,
yearned-for and yearning god.

In the Country of Countries

In these city-filled perspectives
which succeed life, like prisms,
with their blood of time in collected space,
you, consciousness of god, are a fixed present,
the treasure-holding essence of my god,
with all the ages
of colors, music, voices,
in a country of countries.

And in them, simultaneous
belief in fixed paradises of depth,
you succeed yourself, consciousness and god
intercalated with new greenery,
with sun-colored girls,
with brass instruments holding back in long farewell,
which compose your wonted total season,
your timelessness so realized in me.

Harmonious council, city rich
in graduated architectures that I decipher
from above, with rested eyes;
music, cubical vision of succeeding whites
in which the body-soul
sets its contrasted oasis of returning,
of returning, returning, and returning,
with melodious life in every step.
The harps of optic gladness,
god; the conscious planes of glories
possible to this established base of love.

What an opening of roses' lips,
the rosy lips, in these petals
practicable to the enamoured eye
that finds its rest repeatable

in the two infinities; such a possible
existing, my existing
in sufficient being here my whole life long!

Heart of a rose constructed
between you, god desirous of my life,
and me, desirous of yours.

292

By So Many Pilgrims

God in all truth, you fall upon the world,
like a full kiss from a full, open face,
in clear satisfaction of all desires.
The noonday light
is naught but your absolute splendor;
and even its darkest hiding places
you permeate with yourself,
with joy in the lofty possession of life.

Your being beside me
is your natural sequence; and you are
my open mirror in an immense embrace
(the mirror where one is more than oneself),
that left your reflection joined to my reflection,
my image to your image,
in an ember of fused plenitude.

This is the decisive act
of my imagination in motion,
which I considered one day on the sea,
on the sea of my life and of my death,
the sea of my awaited resolution;
and this is the mirage
attained from the most direct road
of my destined desire.

Through this miracle of destiny,
within the forest of my springtime,
crosses the electric current
of beauty pursued by me,
beauty that returned, returns and will return;
the growing succession of my ecstasy of glory.
This is glory, glory only equal to this,
your glory in me, my glory in you.

God; this is the sum in song of those in the paradise
hoped for by so many pilgrims.

293
Of Company and Hour

You dismissed, god, my bird of dawn,
of the dawn of my soul with wakeful body,
in the fog of the pale greenness of spring;
and you are here with me now, reminding us,
with folded wings,
so happy to have awakened me early
with your song of love at sunrise.

You are in everything at every hour,
always fulfilled with having been fulfilled,
with having filled me with yourself,
with having filled me with myself;
and my constant joy in your filling me with you,
is your god-like life;
and your constant joy in my filling myself with you
is my god-like life, my life, life!

How well do our veins communicate!
through you the sun flows between us;
the sun of sea, the sun of fire, flows,
the sun of air, the sun of sun and love,

this sun of love, with the sun of the earth;
and love, love alone and complete flows between us,
flows rich and full, one between the two!

God, love flows, delicious, fragrant,
singing it flows, touching and watching,
because you are my flower, my fruit in my shape,
because you are my mirror in my thought
(thought, shape, mirror, fruit and flower, and all one)
because you are my music, god, of all the world,
all the music of all the world with nothingness.

My music of the bird of dawn today,
now silent with the dawn, absorbed
in what is left of company and hour,
for all my day of confident staying;
this going back and forth from that to mine, from mine
        to that,
with you, who wait for me always, always, always
with folded wings,
after all.

294

I Am Animal of Depth

"In the depth of air" (I said) "I am,"
(I said) "I am animal of depth of air" (on earth),
now on the sea; passed, like the air, through a sun
that is coal above, my outside, and illumines for me
with its coal the second destined space.

But you, god, you also are in this depth
and see by this light, come from another star;

you are here and you are
the greatness and the smallness that I am,
in my very own proportions,
infinite to a depth
that is the sacred well of my own self.

And you were in this well before
with the flower, the swallow, the bull,
and the water; with the dawn
in a crimson arrival of fully renewed life;
with the sunset, in a golden, fleeting glory.
In this daily well you were with me,
with me child, maid, adult, and I was drowning
without knowing you, drowning without thinking
      of you.
This well that was, no more, no less,
than the center of the earth and its life.

And you were in the magic well the destiny
of all the destinies of lovely sensuousness
that knows that to enjoy in plenitude
of loving consciousness
is the greatest virtue that transcends us.

Thus you were to make me think you were you,
to make me feel that I was you,
to make me joy that you were I,
to make me cry that I was I,
in the depth of the air where I am,
where I am animal of depth of air
with wings that do not fly in air,
that fly in light of consciousness
greater than all the dream
of eternities and infinities
that are to be, with no more than I today, of the air.

DIOS DESEADO Y DESEANTE (1949)

295
And in Gold Always the Head Held Alert

Each morning I view the city
where I found you fully, god, essence,
consciousness, you, total beauty.
I see it open with the green-spumed wake
the constant, clean, green-spumed wake
that pushes me taking pleasure in having
space and time to come with me;
that points out to me while pursuing me
my sure road of coming. The city . . .

(No, the roads were not only dusty,
as I said,
of such hot thirst and so many times,
the road that my feet tread
is trod also by rosy gentle feet,
of light of the deserted infinite,
white and green, like a rainy April,
is its serene harassment.)

... In open endlessness there, yes, there,
in a magical breaking up of lights,
is your awakening, city crossed
with crosses, large crosses of ambulation,
with the eagerness of feet and arms and hands;
and in the crimson sun always head alert
to north, to west, to east, to south,
the four golds of the permanent entrance,
the exit with return.

Your head, city; your eyes, your ears,
your sense of smell, with touch and tongue in soul that I
        have seen,
that I looked at, smelled, heard, touched, tasted
with emotion continually contained
in changing of infinities!

296

The Footsteps of the Essence that I Found

In this open wake they fly to my firm being and
        distend my
heart so full of truths, footsteps of the essence that
I found with my consciousness yearning for the lovely
        god.

All those who suffered from hope recognized me for
        the
light already mine, the light that the god fulfilled
        enkindles
in the one who most desires him and desires it.

Along his wake they come, the one and the other, all
        come

230

in immense green and white arm, that fatal arm of him
    who knew
the most, with his definite conviction, of choosing and
    loving.

297

The Heart of All the Body

I went and came with you, god, among that high sea
of unanimous hands, the unanimous ground swell of
arms; arms, hands, the boughs of the trunk, with root of
veins, from the heart of the whole body, which you gather in your land; and all in flame, in shadow, in light,
also in cold; in green and brown, in white and black; in
smelling, looking, tasting, touching and hearing of so
many confused lines.

In enjoyment of a hundred confused lines, I went
and came with you, god, with you.

298

Total Breath of Our Entire Glory

When you arise in sun, god attained,
you are not only in your dawning;
you are in your setting,
in my north, in my south;
you are, with all shades of a scarlet face,
interior and complete,
that looks inward
in the totality of time and space.

And I am inside it,
inside your general consciousness I am
and I am your secret, your diamond,
your greatest treasure, your most affectionate entity.

And I am your bowels
and within them I move
as in air, and I never am your drowned one;
I shall never drown in your nest
as a child never smothers in the womb
of his mother, its yielding nebula;
because you are this blood of mine,
and you are its flowing,
my complete inspiration
and my inspiration complete;
the total breath of our entire glory.

299

You Are Always Falling toward My Lodestone

You pass in the sea, in the sea teeming with all beauties, you, attained god of the sea, of my sea.

You are the future one, and what will follow you; what will always come, he who will always come; for you are abstract desire, the one that never ends, because the memory of you is life as much as you.

Yes; in mass of revealing truth, of perpetual succession you pass, in mass of color, of light, of rhythm; in density of love you pass and pass, you come and come, you are present always; you pass and pass in me; you are the limitlessness of my orbit.

And I stop hurrying, because in the horizon of eternal space you are always descending toward my magnetic pole. Your progression is not flight from what is mine, it is impetuous coming from what is yours, from the whole that you are, eternally enjoying the whole; wayfarer and highway by virtue of the past, by virtue of the present, by virtue of the future.

RÍOS QUE SE VAN (1951–1953)

300

This Immense Atlantic

Solitude is lonely.
And only the lone one finds it
on finding the lonely wave
in the lone sea moving in.

INDEX OF TITLES AND FIRST LINES
Spanish

Abril: 29
¡Abril! ¿solo, desnudo: 150
Acariciar el hombro: 165
Acción: 107
¡Adiós, tú—yo, yo mismo—, que te quedas: 155
A Dios en primavera: 161
—¡Ahí va! 97
Ahora, ¡qué tranquilo: 135
Ahora, soñar es verte: 100
Ahora es cuando he cometido: 77
Aire azul con sol azul: 195
Al abrir hoy los ojos: 135
A la divina luz de las estrellas: 64
A la luna del arte: 45
Alameda: 49
A la puente del amor: 109
Al centro rayeante: 210
Alegra, titiritero: 23
¡Alegre y milagroso vencimiento: 68
Al entrar nuestro coche por el puente grande: 148
Allá va el olor: 28
Alrededor de la copa: 137
Al soneto con mi alma: 59
Amanecer de agosto: 82
A Miranda, en el estadio: 99
¡Amor! . . .: 66
Amor, rosa encendida: 93
amor es, entre tú y yo, El: 115
*Animal de fondo: 203

* Major works by Juan Ramón Jiménez are designated by an asterisk.

Anochecido, grandes nubes ahogan el pueblo: 43
ansioso, El: 185
Ante mí estás, sí: 114
Anteotoño: 143
Anteprimavera: 37
Anunciación: 48
Anunciación: 136
Apartamiento: 49
Aquella que creí gloria cerrada: 110
¡Aquí está! ¡Venid todos! 129
Árboles hombres: 201
Argamasilla del mar: 95
Arias tristes: 3
Arranco de raíz la mata: 123
Arriba canta el pájaro: 151
Arte menor: 37
Asno blanco; verde y ama-: 20
A ti he llegado, riomar: 220
Aun la luna, encallada ya en el día: 106
Aún la luna creciente: 55
A un poeta, para un libro no escrito: 46
—¡Aunque me olvide de mí mismo: 126
Aurora, mayo, vida: 183
Auroras de Moguer: 143
Auroras de Moguer: 148
Auroras de Moguer: 156
Ausencia de un día: 100
ausente, La: 162
A veces, siento: 139
¡Ay, deshacerme: 136
¡Ay, el aire yerto: 138
¡Ay, frente mía, apriétate: 125
Ayer tarde: 201
azul relativo, El: 171

Bajo al jardín. ¡Son mujeres! 9
Baladas de primavera: 27
Belleza (en verso): 147
Blanco, primero, de un blanco: 83

Cada mañana veo la ciudad: 229
Cada otoño, la vida: 122
¡Calla! Gusta el cenit: 116
campo duerme, temblando, El: 13
*Canción: 159
Canción: 96
Canción: 114
Canción: 117
Canción: 117
Canción: 151
Canción corta, canción corta: 132
Canción de invierno: 54
*Canciones de la nueva luz: 175
Canción nocturna: 28
Cantan. Cantan: 54
Cavaré desde la aurora: 86
Cenit: 157
chamariz en el chopo, El: 29
Cielo: 90
Cielo: 95
cielo, en el olvido, El: 128
Cielo, palabra: 90
cielo corre entre lo verde, El: 186
cielo pesa lo mismo, El: 199
Cierra, cierra la puerta: 162
Cobré la rienda: 113
¿Cómo, muerte, tenerte: 140
Como en el ala el infinito vuelo: 59
¿Cómo era, Dios mío, cómo era? 60
Como médanos de oro: 125
Como médanos de oro: 164
¡Cómo no somos únicos! 127
Como piedra en un pozo: 115
¿Cómo pondré en la hora: 75
¿Cómo una voz de afuera: 78
¡Cómo vivo en la llama! 153
Conciencia de hondo azul del día, hoy: 211
Conciencia hoy azul: 211
Conciencia plena: 209

Con la cruz del sur: 214
Con mi mitad allí: 222
Con todos los corazones: 84
Con tu piedra: 199
Convalecencia: 86
corazón de todo el cuerpo, El: 231
corazón roto, El: 61
cordero balaba dulcemente, El: 58
Coronaba la tarde mi tristeza: 67
Creador segundo: 176
creador sin escape, El: 178
¡Crearme, recrearme, vaciarme, hasta: 149
Creemos los nombres: 46
Creía ya perdido: 157
Creímos que todo estaba: 25
Creí que el pobre corazón ya estaba: 61
Cruz del sur se echa en una nube, La: 214
Cual la brisa, recuerdas: 74
Cuando el aire, suprema compañía: 173
Cuando ella se ha ido: 76
Cuando la mujer está: 11
Cuando sales en sol, dios conseguido: 231
Cuando te enciendes, faro de mi alma: 112
Cuando tus manos eran luna: 114
Cuán estraños: 111
Cuatro: 165
cuerpo tiene más hambre, ¿El: 79
Cuesta arriba: 127

De compaña y de hora: 226
¿De dónde es una hoja: 144
¡Deja chorrear tu beso: 116
Dejé el sí que lo enterraran: 80
De la noche ha saltado. Y yo le digo: 171
Delante está el carmín de la emoción: 170
De nuestros movimientos naturales: 204
Deprisa, tierra, deprisa: 77
De pronto, un raro vacío: 76

De tanto caminar por los alcores: 66
Desde dentro: 167
Despertar: 92
Desvelo: 138
*Diario de un poeta reciéncasado: 87
día vendrá un hombre, Un: 146
¡Días, días, días, días! 78
Días nulos, cual los días: 179
Diluvio: 121
Dios del venir, te siento entre mis manos: 203
*Dios deseado y deseante: 229
Dios en conciencia, caes sobre el mundo: 225
Dios está azul. La flauta y el tambor: 27
Dios primero: 179
¿Dónde está la palabra, corazón: 153
¿Dónde se han escondido los colores: 35
Doraba la luna el río: 14
Dormidos: nuestro cuerpo: 156
dormir es como un puente, El: 163

Eco: 47
Elejía: 71
*Elejías: 31
Ellos: 52
Ellos: 152
Ellos: 162
En amoroso llenar: 217
"En el fondo de aire" (dije) "estoy": 227
En el naranjo está la estrella: 181
*En el otro costado: 193
En el recuerdo estás tal como estabas: 222
En el viento azul se van: 81
En esta abierta estela vuelan hacia mi fijo estar: 230
En estas perspectivas ciudadales: 224
En igualdad segura de espresión: 215
En la circumbre: 221
En la ciudad de piedra, húmeda y solitaria: 41
En la noche tranquila: 153

En la roca: 176
En lo mejor que tengo: 218
En mar pasas: 232
En mi tercero mar: 205
En mi tercero mar estabas tú: 205
En país de países: 224
Ente: 200
Entre la arboladura serena y la alta nube: 213
Entre las nubes abiertas: 184
En un centro: 187
Epitafio de mí, vivo: 110
Epitafio ideal: 150
Era—¡no, no era asi!—de otra manera: 69
Era tan bello como en sueños: 119
Eres tan bella: 111
Esa órbita abierta: 216
escursión, La: 184
Es el pueblo. Por encima: 22
Esparce octubre, al blando movimiento: 72
¡Espera, luz, espera! 109
Esperanza: 70
¡Esperar! ¡Esperar! Mientras, el cielo: 70
Estaba echado yo en la tierra, enfrente: 62
*estación total I, La: 167
*estación total II, La: 189
Esta conciencia que me rodeó: 208
Estado: 169
Está el árbol en flor: 111
Esta gracia sin nombre ni apellido: 89
Estampa de invierno: 35
Estas cayendo siempre hasta mi imán: 232
Este inmenso Atlántico: 233
. . . ¡Este instante: 90
Este instante: 124
Este otro yo que espía: 182
*Estío: 73
Estoy completo de naturaleza: 168
Estoy viviendo: 175
Estoy viviendo. Mi sangre: 175

Estrellas, estrellas dulces: 8
estrella venida, La: 181
*Eternidades: 107

felicidad, La: 179
Figuraciones: 157
flores bajo el rayo, Las: 177
flores se dan la mano, Las: 177
Flor que vuelve: 172
¡Forjadores: 113
forma que me queda, La: 213
**frente pensativa, La*: 53
Fría es la noche y pura: 57
Frío nuevo: canta un gallo: 154
fruta de mi flor, La: 208
Fuente seca y ruinosa, ¡ya no eras más que piedra! 34
Fuera: 138
gallardete, blanco, El: 103
Gracia: 89
Gracias, vida, porque he sabido: 176
¡Granados en cielo azul! 17

Ha sido igual que otro: 135
He llegado a una tierra de llegada: 219
Hojas nuevas: 40
Hombre solo: 68
¡Horas, ruinas doradas: 119
Huir azul: 186

Iberia: 105
¡Iberia de oro, que entreveo ya en la bruma: 105
Igual, la flor retorna: 172
Igual que una espada pura: 75
¡Inmenso almendro en flor: 127
Inmortalidad: 139
¡Instante, sigue, sé recuerdo: 124

jardín, El: 69
*Jardines lejanos: 9

*Laberinto: 41
Latitud: 154
Libro: 129
¡Libro, afán: 129
Limpio iré a ti: 112
Lo que corre por la tierra es humo: 182
Lujo: 179
luna de cristal va, verde, clara, nueva, La: 34
luna me echa en el alma, La: 8
Luz tú: 188
Luz vertical: 188
Luz y negro: 177
Lloré, lloré, lloré hasta ahogar el mundo: 121
Llueve sobre el río . . .: 37

Madrugada: 10
Madrugada: 128
Madrugada: 154
Mañana de la cruz: 27
mano contra la luz, La: 142
Mar: 94
mar de olas de cinc y espumas, El: 91
Mar despierto: 102
Mares: 130
Mariposa de luz: 132
Mariposa malva: 97
Mariposa malva: 97
Mar verde y cielo gris y cielo azul: 218
Me adelanté el corazón: 83
Me adorné el corazón: 117
Me colmó el sol del poniente: 117
Me despediste, dios, mi pájaro del alba: 226
Me desperté debajo: 151
*Melancolía: 43
Me metí en el arbusto: 40
¡Memoria inmensa mía: 124
Mi alma es hermana del cielo: 5
Mi casa: 184
Mientras te quede a ti esta sola hoja: 114

Mi lágrima y la estrella: 134
¡Mi plata aquí en el sur, en este sur: 222
¡Mira, por los chopos: 40
¡Mira la amapola: 179
¡Miranda, Miranda, Miranda: 99
Mi reino: 178
¡Mis pies! ¡qué hondos en la tierra! 113
Mi tedio se repite en la corriente: 71
Mi triste ansia: 182
momento, El: 134
Monotonía: 91
Morí en el sueño: 110
Movimiento: 187
Muerto que duerme: 166
Mujer, ¡ay, chamarasca! 158
mujer, con la música, La: 145
música, La: 153
Música fiel en escala: 198
Muy buenas tardes, aldea: 16

Nada me importa esta muerte: 158
¿Nada todo? ¿Pues y este gusto entero: 140
¡Necio yo! ¿Cómo: 152
negro toro solo surje, neto y bello, El: 143
Niño último: 198
noche, La: 111
noche, La: 163
Noches ideales: 64
Nocturno: 134
Nocturno soñado: 131
No es negra: 183
No eres: 79
No eres: 79
No más soñar; pensar: 101
No quise más la estrella: 139
No sé con qué decirlo: 107
No sólo estás entre los hombres: 204
No somos más que un débil saco: 142

¡No te vayas, recuerdo, no te vayas! 125
No vi cielo más alto: 156
¡Nube blanca: 145
Nube diamante: 185
Nunca creí que el albo lirio fuera: 63

obra, La: 155
Octubre: 62
¡Oh, cuán despierto tú, mar rico: 102
¡Oh dicha sin razón! 120
¡Oh recuerdo, sé yo! 126
¡Oh tiempo, dame tu secreto: 110
—¡Oh voluntad tardia! 92
Olvidanzas: 25
Órdenes: 183
Oro mío: 104
¡Oro nuevo: 37
otoñado, El: 168
Otoño: 72
Otoño corporal: 158
otra tarde, se ha llevado, ¡La: 6
otro éste, El: 182

pajarito verde, El: 153
pájaro del agua, El: 159
Pájaro del agua: 159
pájaros del aire, Los: 216
pájaros de yo sé donde, Los: 193
¡Palabra mía eterna! 122
Pasan todas, verdes, granas . . .: 73
pasos de la entraña que encontré, Los: 230
Pastorales: 13
Patria: 144
Perro divino: 129
perro está ladrando a mi conciencia, ¿El: 215
Piedra y cielo: 123
pino se consuela, El: 169
Pintor que me has pintado: 54
plenitud, La: 170

244

Plenitud de hoy, es: 107
poema, El: 123
Poemas agrestes: 39
Poemas impersonales: 45
Poemas májicos y dolientes: 35
¡Poesía; rocío: 141
Poesía (en verso): 137
Poeta y palabra: 173
Por el fondo negro: 162
Por tanto peregrino: 225
Preguntas al residente: 196
Presente: 37
Primavera: 65
Primera: 196
Primer almendro en flor: 88
Puerto: 156
Pureza: 55

¡Qué alegre, en primavera: 85
¡Qué cerca ya del alma: 87
¡Qué inmensa desgarradura: 123
¿Qué le pasa a una música: 144
¿Qué me importa, sol seco? 176
¡Qué mina ésta de mi luz: 177
Que nada me invada de fuera: 188
¡Que se me va, que se me va, que se me va! 134
¿Qué soledad, qué yermo? 176
Quién anda por el camino: 12
Quien fuera no me vió, me vió su sombra: 189
¡Quién sabe del revés de cada hora! 53
¡Quiero dormir, esta noche: 155
Quiero llegar a mi fin: 185
Quisiera clavarte, hora: 84
Quisiera que mi libro: 136

Raíces y alas. Pero que las alas arraiguen: 88
recuerdo, El: 164
recuerdo I, El: 124

recuerdo II, El: 125
recuerdo III, El: 125
recuerdo V, El: 126
recuerdo se va, El: 51
Redondez: 165
Remanso: 115
Respiración total de nuestra entera gloria: 231
Retorno fugaz: 60
Rey de vanidades: 67
Río de cristal, dormido: 3
Río-mar-desierto: 220
río pasa por debajo, El: 126
Ríos que se van: 233
ritmo, El: 164
ritmo, El: 183
Ritmo de ola: 185
Romances de Coral Gables: 199
Rompió mi alma con oro: 167
rosa, La: 180
Rosa, la rosa . . . (Pero aquella rosa . . .): 191
Rosa de sombra: 189
rosa huele con su olor más fino, La: 65
Rosa íntima: 191
Rosas: 128
—Rueda de niñas. Frájil coro: 49
Ruta: 130

sabor, ¡El: 180
Sé bien que soy tronco: 120
sendero se ha dormido, El: 15
Señor, matadme si queréis: 161
Sentido y elemento: 180
Sé que mi obra es lo mismo: 147
ser uno, El: 188
Será lo mismo: 152
Se va la noche, negro toro: 138
Se va subiendo a lo otro: 200
¡Sí! 80
Sí—dice el día—: 133

Sí. La Mancha, de agua: 95
¡Sí, sed, sed, sed horrible! 115
Siento que el barco mío: 130
¡Si fuera yo como un lugar: 154
Sima estraña: 195
Sin nubes ya: 187
Sin tedio ni descanso: 212
Si vas de prisa: 118
Si yo he salido tanto al mundo: 212
sol dorará las hojas, El: 21
soledad está sola, La: 233
soledad sonora, La: 33
Sol en el camarote: 93
Sol en el camarote: 101
¡Soles de auroras nuevas contra los viejos muros: 82
solo amigo, El: 152
Sólo en lo eterno podría: 178
Sólo tú me acompañas, sol amigo: 86
¡Sólo un punto! 94
¡Sol quincallero: 143
sombra parece, La: 74
Sonetos espirituales: 59
¿Sostiene la hoja seca: 141
Soy animal de fondo: 227
Soy como un niño distraído: 121
¿Soy yo quien anda, esta noche: 10
Suavidad: 141
Sueña, sueña mientras duermes: 118
¡Sueño, muerte: 144

Tal como estabas: 222
¡Tan bien como se encuentra: 115
Tarde en ninguna parte: 90
Te conocí, porque al mirar la huella: 112
Te deshojé, como una rosa: 96
Te he dado, sol insomne, latido por latido: 45
Te tenía olvidado: 95
¡Tesoros del azul: 133
tierra lleva por la tierra, La: 131

Tira la piedra de hoy: 164
Toda la noche: 193
Todas las nubes arden: 207
Todas las nubes arden: 207
todo interno, El: 219
Todo para ellos, todo, todo: 52
Todos duermen, abajo: 130
Todos vamos, tranquilos, trabajando: 217
trasparencia, Dios, la trasparencia, La: 203
Trastorno: 63
Trasunto de cristal: 48
tres, Los: 103
tres, Los: 144
Tres le dieron yel: 165
Tronco como el aire: 187
Tú: 73
Tú, palabra de mi boca, animada: 139
Tu amor—¡qué alegre! 128
Tu desnudez: 180
Tú estás, dios deseado, en la circumbre: 221
Tú estás entre los cúmulos: 210
Tú me llevas, conciencia plena, deseante dios: 209
Tuvo un instante, dulce rosa: 84

Una a una, las hojas secas van cayendo: 31

Valle tranquilo: 166
Vamos entrando en oro. Un oro puro: 104
Vé donde la aurora: 183
vencedor oculto, El: 175
verdad, La: 141
Verde verderol: 29
Verde verderol: 29
viaje definitivo, El: 39
Vida: 110
Vida, gracias, muerte: 176
Vida segunda, ésta: 135
viento rinde las ramas, El: 10
viento se ha llevado las nubes de tristeza, El: 33

Vino, primero pura: 108
¡Voz mía, canta, canta: 142

¡*Ya*! 106
Ya están ahí las carretas . . .: 18
Ya la nieve ha dejado al sol: 97
Y en oro siempre la cabeza alerta: 229
Yo estaba triste, y le aullaba: 47
Yo fuí y vine contigo, dios: 231
Yo le he ganado ya al mundo: 141
Yo le tiré al ideal: 26
Yo no quería vencerte: 163
Yo no sé cómo saltar: 85
Yo no seré yo, muerte: 157
Yo no volveré: 7
Yo no volveré. Y la noche: 7
¡Yo sólo vivo dentro: 96
. . . Y yo me iré. Y se quedarán los pájaros: 39

INDEX OF TITLES AND FIRST LINES
English

Above, the bird is singing: 151
Absent One, The: 162
Action: 107
All are asleep, below: 130
All night long: 193
All others pass by, green, red . . .: 73
All the Clouds Are Burning: 207
All the clouds are burning: 207
All things for them, all, all: 52
Along the black depth: 162
Already the snow has left open to the sun: 97
Among the open clouds: 184
. . . And I shall go. And the birds will go on singing: 39
And in Gold Always the Head Held Alert: 229
Annunciation: 48
Annunciation: 136
Anxious One, The: 185
April: 29
April! Alone, unsaddled: 150
Around the crown: 137
As in the wing infinite flight exists: 59
Asleep: our body: 156
As long as you have left this one petal: 114
As the stagecoach enters town by the large bridge: 148
At times I feel: 139
August Daybreak: 82
Autumn: 72
Autumn Fruit: 168
Awakening: 92

Being One: 188
Beneath the divine light of heaven's stars: 64
Between the poised masts and spars and the high cloud: 213
Birds from I Know Where, The: 193
birds of the air, The: 216
Blue air with blue sunlight: 195
Blue Flight: 186
blue titmouse in the poplar, The: 29
Books: 129
Book: 129
Brief Return: 60
Brief song, brief song: 132
Broken Heart, The: 61
butterfly of light, A: 132
By So Many Pilgrims: 225

Cast off the rock of today: 164
Circumsummit: 221
Clean I shall come: 112
Close, close the door: 162
Cloudless now: 187
Cold is the night and pure: 57
Condition: 169
Consciousness Blue Today: 211
Consciousness of the deep blue of the day, today: 211
Convalescence: 86
Corporeal Autumn: 158
countryside sleeps, trembling, The: 13
crystal moon is moving, green, clear, and new, The: 34

Dawn, May, Life: 183
Daybreak: 128
Days, days, days, days! 78
dead sleeping, The: 166
Dear Lord, kill me if Thou wilt: 161
Definitive Voyage: 39
Deluge: 121
Diamond cloud: 185

251

Divine Hound: 129
Does the withered leaf hold: 141
Doomed Creator: 178
Dream, dream, while you sleep: 118
Dreamed Nocturne: 131
Dried up, ruined fountain, you are now but a rock! 34
Dusk: 183

Each morning I view the city: 229
Early Morning: 10
Early Morning: 154
Earth carries us through earth: 131
Echo: 47
Elegy: 71
Entity: 200
Epitaph of Me, Living: 110
evening crowned my doleful discontent, The: 67
Evening Nowhere: 90
Every autumn life: 122
Everything nothing? And what of this full pleasure: 140
Excursion, The: 184

Faithful, the flower returns: 172
Faithful music in the scale: 198
Faster, earth, faster: 77
Figurations: 157
First almond tree in bloom: 88
First question: 196
flowers hold hands, The: 177
Flowers under Lightning: 177
Foolish I! How: 152
Footsteps of the Essence That I Found, The: 230
Forgers: 113
Form Left to Me, The: 213
For one moment of delight: 84
Four: 165
From so much walking on the bitter hills: 66
From Within: 167

Fruit of My Flower, The: 208
Full Consciousness: 209

Garden, The: 69
Gay and miraculous self-mastery: 68
Gentleness: 141
Gladden, gladden, puppet-player: 23
God First: 179
God in all truth, you fall upon the world: 225
God is bright blue. Now the flute and the drum: 27
God of what is to come, I feel you in my hands: 203
Golden Iberia that I glimpse now through the mist: 105
Good-bye to you—to me, myself—left behind: 155
good evening to you, village, A: 16
Go where the dawn: 183
Grace: 89
Green Greenfinch: 29
Green greenfinch: 29
Green sea and gray sky and blue sky: 218

Hand Against the Light: 142
Happiness: 179
Heart of All the Body, The: 231
Here it is! Come all! 129
Hidden Victor, The: 175
Hope: 70
Hours, golden ruins: 119
How, death, am I to fear: 140
How can I place in time: 75
How close now to the soul: 87
How does an outer voice: 78
How gay it is, in spring: 85
How I live in the flame! 153
How strange: 111
How we are not alone! 127
Hush now! Savor the zenith: 116

I Am Animal of Depth: 227
I am fulfilled with nature: 168

253

I am like an inattentive child: 121
I am losing it, losing it, losing it! 134
I awoke beneath: 151
Iberia: 105
Ideal Epitaph: 150
Ideal Nights: 64
I did not wish to subdue: 163
I died in sleep: 110
I do not know how to leap: 85
I embellished my heart: 117
I feel this boat of mine: 130
If I have gone so much about the world: 212
I fired at the ideal: 26
If I were only like a bit: 154
If you hurry: 118
I gave you, sleepless sun, one heartbeat at a time: 45
I go to the garden. Women! 9
I grasped the reins: 113
I had believed that my poor heart had been: 61
I had forgotten you: 95
I have arrived at a land of arrival: 219
I have arrived beside you, river-sea: 220
I have no words to say it: 107
I have now won from the world: 141
I know I am the trunk: 120
I know my work is the same: 147
I lay upon the earth, my eyes upon: 62
I left the yes to be interred: 80
I Live: 175
I live. And my blood: 175
Imitation Sea: 95
Immense flowering almond tree: 127
Immense memory of mine: 124
Immortality: 139
Immortal word of mine! 122
In Equality Sure of Expression: 215
I never saw a higher sky: 156
I never thought the snow-white lily could: 63
In front is emotion's crimson hue: 170

In Loving Fulfillment: 217
In my memory you are just as you were: 222
In My Third Sea: 205
In my third sea you were: 205
I no longer wanted the star: 139
In One Center: 187
Instant, endure, be a memory: 124
Internal All, The: 219
In the Best I Have: 218
In the blue wind the verses: 81
In the Country of Countries: 224
"In the depth of air" (I said) "I am": 227
In the distance come the ox-carts . . .: 18
In the orange tree is the star: 181
In these city-filled perspectives: 224
In the town of stone, rain-drenched and solitary: 41
In the tranquil night: 153
In this open wake they fly to my firm being: 230
Intimate Rose: 191
I recognized you, for seeing the print: 112
I set my heart ahead: 83
I shall dig from the dawn: 86
I shall not be myself, Death: 157
I Shall Not Return: 7
I shall not return. And night: 7
I should like to impale you, hour: 84
I should like to sleep, this night: 155
Is it I, pacing my room: 10
Is the body hungrier: 79
Is the dog barking at my conscience: 215
I stripped you of petals, like a rose: 96
I thought already lost: 157
It is climbing toward otherness: 200
It rains on the river . . .: 37
It shattered my soul with gold: 167
It sprang from the night. I say to it: 171
It was—No, not thus—but otherwise: 69
It was as lovely as in dreams: 119
It was just like being born: 135

It will be the same: 152
I uproot the bush: 123
I walked into the shrub: 40
I want to reach my end: 185
I was sad, and I howled: 47
I went and came with you, god: 231
I wept, I wept, I wept until I drowned the world: 121
I wish my book might be: 136

Just as You Were: 222

King of Vanities: 67

lamb baaed gently, The: 58
Late one afternoon the wind: 6
Latitude: 154
Let nothing invade me from without: 188
Let us create the names: 46
Let your kisses flow: 116
Life: 110
Life, Thanks, Death: 176
Light and Black: 177
Like an immaculate sword: 75
Like golden dunes of sand: 164
Like pebble in a well: 115
Like the breeze, you remind us: 74
Little Green Bird, The: 153
lone black bull appears, clear, beautiful, The: 143
Look at the poppy: 179
Love . . .! 66
Love, crimson rose: 93
Love is, between you and me: 115
Luxury: 179

Man Alone: 68
Mauve Butterfly: 97
Mauve Butterfly: 97
Memories: 164

Memories are like golden dunes: 125
Men Trees: 201
Miranda, Miranda, Miranda: 99
Moguer Dawns: 143
Moguer Dawns: 148
Moguer Dawns: 156
Moment, The: 134
Monotony: 91
moon, now run aground in day, still, The: 106
moon sends into my deep, The: 8
moon was gilding the river, The: 14
Morning of the Cross: 27
Movement: 187
Music: 153
My Anguish: 182
My boredom is repeated in the stream: 71
My feet, how deeply sunk in earth! 113
My Gold: 104
My House: 184
My Realm: 178
My silver here in the south, in this south: 222
My soul is kin to the gray: 5
My tear and the star: 134

Native Land: 144
Neighborhood Park: 49
New cold: cock crowing: 154
New gold: 37
New Leaves: 40
Night: 111
Night: 163
Nightfall. Large clouds smother the town: 43
Night retreats, black bull: 138
Night Song: 28
Nocturne: 134
No more dreams; to think: 101
Now! 106
Now, to dream is to see you: 100
Now is when I have committed: 77

. . . Now what a tranquil: 135
Null days, like the days: 179

Oh brow of mine, press close: 125
October: 62
October at the bland and gentle blowing: 72
Of Company and Hour: 226
Of Our Natural Movements: 204
Oh, how wide-awake you are, rich sea: 102
Oh, singing rain-bird: 159
Oh, the stiff air: 138
Oh, to be dissolved: 136
O joy without reason! 120
Oh memory, be I! 126
Once when your hands were moon: 114
One by one the dry leaves are falling: 31
One day a man will come: 146
One Day's Absence: 100
One Friend, The: 152
Only I live within: 96
Only in eternity could: 178
Only one moment! 94
Only you are with me, friendly sun: 86
On the Rock: 176
O painter who painted me: 54
Opus: 155
Orders: 183
—O tardy will! 92
O time, tell me your secret: 110
Outside: 138

path has fallen asleep, The: 15
Peak: 187
Perfectly though my soul: 115
pine consoles itself, The: 169
Please do not leave, remembrance, do not leave! 125
Plenitude: 170
Plenitude of today is: 107
Poem, The: 123

Poet and Word: 173
Poetry; dew: 141
Pomegranates against blue sky! 17
Port: 156
Pre-Autumn: 143
Present, The: 37
Pre-Spring: 37

Questions to the Resident: 196
Quiet Water: 115

Rain-Bird, The: 159
Relative Blue: 171
Remembrance I: 124
Remembrance II: 125
Remembrance III: 125
Remembrance V: 126
Remembrance goes: 51
Returning Flower: 172
Rhythm: 164
Rhythm: 183
—Ring of little girls. Fragile, white: 49
river is flowing under, The: 126
River of crystal, asleep: 3
River-Sea-Desert: 220
Roots and wings. But let the wings grow roots: 88
rose, The: 180
Rose, the rose . . . (But that one rose . . .): 191
rose exhales its most divine bouquet, The: 65
Rose of Shadow: 189
Roses: 128
Roundness: 165

Sea: 94
Seas: 130
Seaway: 130
sea with waves of zinc and swells, The: 91
Second Creator: 176

second life, this, A: 135
See how the golden children climb: 40
Sense and Element: 180
setting sun flooded, The: 117
shadow, it seems, The :74
She first came to me pure: 108
ship's pennant, white, The: 103
Singing. Singing: 54
Sky: 90
Sky: 95
Sky, a word: 90
sky, in the oblivion, The: 128
sky courses through the green, The: 186
sky weighs as much, The: 199
Sleep, death: 144
Sleeping is like a bridge: 163
Solitude is lonely: 233
Song: 96
Song: 114
Song: 117
Song: 117
Song: 151
Southern Cross lies down upon a cloud, The: 214
Spring: 65
Stars, stars, sweet stars: 8
Star That Came, The: 181
Still the crescent moon: 55
Strange Abyss: 195
Suddenly, a strange emptiness: 76
Sun in the Cabin: 93
Sun in the Stateroom: 101
sunlight will gild the leaves, The: 21
Sunrises of new dawns against the ancient walls: 82

Taste: 180
Thanks, life, for I have been able: 176
That Open Orbit: 216
There goes the scent: 28

—There it goes! 97
They: 52
They: 152
They: 162
This consciousness that surrounded me: 208
This death matters not to me—: 158
This grace with neither first nor last name: 89
This Immense Atlantic: 233
. . . This instant: 90
This is the village. Above: 22
This other I that spies: 182
This Other One: 182
Though I forget myself: 126
Three gave him gall: 165
Tin-plated sun: 143
To a Poet for an Unwritten Book: 46
To caress a shoulder: 165
To create, recreate, empty myself, until: 149
Today when I opened my eyes: 135
To God in Spring: 161
To hope! To hope! Meanwhile the sky festoons: 70
To Miranda in the Stadium: 99
Total Breath of Our Entire Glory: 231
To the ancient bridge of love: 109
To the Moon of Art: 45
To the Rayed Center: 210
To the Sonnet with My Soul: 59
Tranquil Valley: 166
Transparence, God, Transparence: 203
Travesty: 63
Treasures of the blue: 133
tree is flowering, The: 111
Trunk like the air: 187
Truth: 141

Ultimate Child: 198
Uphill: 127

Vertical light: 188

Vision in crystal: 48
Voice of mine, sing, sing: 142

—Wait, light, wait! 109
Wakefulness: 138
Wave Rhythm: 185
We are all calmly working: 217
We are entering gold. A pure gold: 104
We are nothing but a feeble bag: 142
We thought that everything was: 25
We Three: 103
We Three: 144
What a mine this of my light: 177
What an immense tearing to shreds: 123
What do I care, dry sun? 176
What floats over the earth is smoke: 182
What happens to a melody: 144
What I believed locked to glory: 110
What is this instant: 124
What solitude, what desert? 176
What was she like, dear God, what was she like? 60
Whence is a leaf: 144
When she has gone away: 76
When the air, supreme companion: 173
When woman is present, all: 11
When you are lighted, beacon of my soul: 112
When you arise in sun, god attained: 231
Where have all the colors gone to hide: 35
Where is the word, heart: 153
White at first, the full white: 83
White cloud: 145
White donkey; yellow and green: 20
Who can know the reverse of any hour? 53
Whoever it was did not see me, his shadow did: 189
Who is walking up the road: 12
Wide-Awake-Sea: 102
wind has swept away the clouds of sadness, The: 33

wind is bending the branches, The: 10
Winter Etching: 35
Winter Song: 54
With all the beloved hearts: 84
With My Half There: 222
Without Tedium nor Rest: 212
With the Southern Cross: 214
With Your Stone: 199
Woman, oh, swift brush fire! 158
Woman, with music: 145

Yes! 80
Yes. La Mancha, as water: 95
Yes—says the day: 133
Yes, thirst, thirst, horrible thirst! 115
Yesterday evening: 201
You: 73
You, word of my mouth, given life: 139
You are, desired god, in the circumsummit: 221
You Are Always Falling toward My Lodestone: 232
You are among the gold: 210
You are as beautiful: 111
You Are Not: 79
You are not: 79
You are not only among men: 204
You bear me, full consciousness, yearning god: 209
You dismissed, god, my bird of dawn: 226
You Light: 188
You pass in the sea: 232
Your love—how gaily: 128
Your Nakedness: 180
You stand before me, yes: 114

Zenith: 157

JUAN RAMÓN JIMÉNEZ

THREE HUNDRED POEMS, 1903–1953

translated by Eloïse Roach

with drawings by Jo Alys Downs

HAS BEEN SET IN ELEVEN POINT GARAMOND LEADED
TWO POINTS AND PRINTED ON SIXTY POUND LOGAN
EGGSHELL PAPER; PRINTED AND BOUND BY THE
UNIVERSITY OF TEXAS PRINTING DIVISION.